Dear

May Hashem answer
all your prayers.

All the best!

Ahava Soray

My Sister, the Jew

My Sister, the Jew

Ahuvah Gray

TARGUM/FELDHEIM

First published 2001
Copyright © 2001 by Ahuvah Gray
ahuvabasyisroel@hotmail.com
www.MySisterTheJew.com
ISBN 1-56871-276-6

Published by:
Targum Press, Inc.
22700 W. Eleven Mile Rd.
Southfield, MI 48034
E-mail: targum@netvision.net.il
Fax toll-free: 888-298-9992

Distributed by:
Feldheim Publishers
200 Airport Executive Park
Nanuet, NY 10954
www.feldheim.com

Printed in Israel

Rabbi Aryeh Carmell
Yeshivat Dvar Yerushalayim

The most famous convert in history was Ruth. As she started her journey to the Land of Israel, Ruth proclaimed: "For where you go, I will go, your people shall be my people and your God — my God."

My Sister, the Jew is the story of an African-American woman who followed in Ruth's footsteps. Ahuvah Gray is the granddaughter of sharecroppers from Mound Bayou, Mississippi. Her grandmother taught her the psalms of David at an early age and she believes that it was this that later in life was instrumental in bringing her to the faith of King David.

The book describes the various ups and downs of her active life until she settled in Israel and ultimately was able to proclaim, like David's great-grandmother Ruth, "Your people shall be my people and your God — my God."

It is my feeling that this book will help both Orthodox and non-Orthodox Jews to develop a new and deeper appreciation of their spiritual roots.

Rabbi Aryeh Carmell

Rabbi Emanuel Feldman

...This is an affecting story of courage, steadfastness, and faith. Uplifting and inspiring, this tale of struggle and triumph offers the reader a fresh appreciation of what it means to become a member of *Am Yisrael*....

Rabbi Emanuel Feldman
editor, *Tradition Magazine*

Rebbetzin Tziporah Heller

Knowing Ahuvah Gray is a spiritual adventure. The drama and sincerity of her search for a way of life in which her mind, spirit, and body are all dancing to the tune of the same fiddler is unforgettable. As a teacher, presenting the great heroines of the Bible has always been a challenge. Our concerns are so petty, and our desire to move forward is sometimes stunted by living in an era in which there are so few heroines. Ahuvah is one of these heroines. Her story cannot fail to inspire us to make our own lives a bit bigger.

Tziporah Heller
lecturer at Neve Yerushalayim and
author of *More Precious than Pearls*

DEDICATION

Honor your father and your mother, as Hashem, your God,
commanded you, so that your days will be lengthened and so
that it will be good for you, upon the land that Hashem, your
God, gives you.

(Devarim 5:16)

I dedicate this book in loving memory of my parents

Sylvester and Christine Franklin Gray

and my youngest brother

Lorenzo Buckner

My parents, of blessed memory, were both alive when I
decided to move to Israel and to become a candidate for
conversion to Judaism. When I advised them of my decision, they gave me their blessings. To quote my mother:

"Whatever you do in life, you should do it with dignity."

Acknowledgments

With gratitude and appreciation I'd like to thank the following people:

My family, Ezra Sr., Oscar, Nellie, and Ezra Jr., whom I've neglected in order to finish this book. Nellie also assisted with the graphic design of this book.

Shmuel Blitz, who encouraged me to start and finish my task.

My warmest appreciation goes to Rabbi and Rebbetzin Heyman, my parents, who took me by the hand from start to finish and nurtured me.

Rabbi Aharon Feldman and Rabbi Leib Heyman, who offered hours of assistance regarding halachic issues.

Yosef Ben Shlomo Hakohen, author of *The Universal Jew*, who acted as my spiritual advisor.

Dr. Avraham and Rochel Schwartzbaum for their encouragement in the early stages of my writing.

Naomi Rosenberg for her editing skills and great sense of humor from start to finish.

My little sister and dearest friend, Batya Ruth Shultz, who spent numerous hours reading.

Many special thanks to the following people for their combined editing skills: Zeev Breier, who prepared the original version of this book; Miriam Levi; Linda Tilghman; Shaina Medwed; Sarah Shapiro; Aviva Rappaport; Sarah Rosenblatt; Devorah Sheril; Shirley Martin; and Ruthie and Tzvi Aryeh Ingber.

All my friends from the various seminaries throughout Yerushalayim who gave me the stamina to keep the story alive. My warmest regards to all the women who kept my dream alive by sponsoring parlor meetings, especially Faigie Langsam and Elaine Lehman.

Ruth Broyde-Sharon for her impressive talents and editing skills.

My *chavrusa*, Ruthie Hamaoui, who learned with me every Wednesday while she was studying at Michlalah.

Professor Yaakov Meir Mann for his *tefillos*.

All the women in the neighborhood who sent the leftover *cholent* that nourished my body and soul.

A very special thanks to all the staff at Targum.

Lastly, my family and dear friends, the Frohweins, who have loved me and walked with me through my fears.

Above all, I would like to express my gratitude to Hashem for giving me the strength to walk through all my challenges in life.

"One who walks with the wise will grow wise" (*Mishlei* 18:20).

FOREWORD

by Ruth Broyde-Sharon

B orn in Chicago, the granddaughter of sharecroppers from Mound Bayou, Mississippi, raised as a Christian, Delores Gray followed a highly unlikely path from airline stewardess to minister, then tour guide, and finally to Orthodox Jew now living in Jerusalem.

How does one make sense of this journey? What were the spiritual pushes and pulls along the way that could explain this radical metamorphosis?

When African-American Delores Gray says she feels she was present at Mount Sinai and was one of the original Jews to receive the 613 mitzvos, her Christian friends are bewildered. Originally a born-again Christian who was first licensed as a minister at the Strait-Way House of Worship in Los Angeles and ordained as a minister at the International Assemblies of God in San Diego, Delores now prays in Hebrew three times a day, keeps kosher, and lives in Bayit Vegan, an Orthodox Jewish neighborhood in Jerusalem.

Ostracized by many of her born-again Christian friends, denounced by others for "trafficking with the devil," Delores has not wavered from her course. Once a nonbeliever, as her mother described Delores as a young girl, today her life is informed and affected on the most intimate level by her belief in the Creator. She prays daily for vision and clarity, as a Jew, to perform God's will.

The first time Delores visited Jerusalem, she knew instantaneously that it would become her home, and that she would leave everyone and everything behind if necessary to fulfill that vision.

How could a person so sheltered by family and friends take such a perilous step that would cut her off forever from her roots? How could she abandon her religious heritage and her homeland? Unlike Ruth of the Bible, Delores had no Naomi to cling to, no Naomi to lead the way as she changed her home, her people, and her God.

What she did have was her God and the people He provided for her – strangers who became her guides, her friends, and ultimately her new family. *My Sister, the Jew* is the story of Delores's amazing journey to Zion, a journey full of thorns and nettles, but a journey that ultimately transformed Delores to Ahuvah, a daughter of Israel.

Ruth Broyde-Sharon

Journalist, Documentary Filmmaker, Interior Decorator

The faith of your times will be the strength of your salvations, wisdom and knowledge; fear of Hashem — that is man's treasure.

(Yeshayah 33:6)

Each of the six words in the beginning half of this verse corresponds to one of the six orders of the Mishnah. The highest level of all, however, is *yiras Hashem*, fear of God. This is the greatest treasure mankind has.

(based on an explanation given by Rabbi Aaron Feldman)

Introduction

Hashem said to Abram, "Go for yourself [lecha] from your land, from your birthplace, and from your father's house, to the land that I will show you."

(Genesis 12:1)

The word lecha denotes "for your benefit and for your own advantage."

(Rashi)

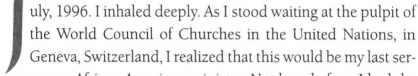

J uly, 1996. I inhaled deeply. As I stood waiting at the pulpit of the World Council of Churches in the United Nations, in Geneva, Switzerland, I realized that this would be my last sermon as an African-American minister. Not long before, I had decided to become a Jew.

The event was organized to honor the fiftieth anniversary of UNICEF and UNESCO being held together with the UN Commission on Human Rights Sub-Commission. Wilda Spalding, an indefatigable organizer and a nongovernmental leader at the United Nations for twenty-five years, had invited my dear friend Ruth Broyde-Sharon and myself to participate as nongovernmental official observer-delegates and to speak at a round table discussion on the effects of racism and intolerance.

This Sunday morning, at the religious service, my audience at the World Council of Churches included others from our U.S. delegation as well as United Nations personnel and local residents of Geneva. It was a mixed crowd from diverse religious backgrounds.

My eyes scanned the audience as I tried to assess the needs of the group. I wanted to speak openly, without alienating them. I had to find just the right words to engage their hearts.

I had been introduced as a Christian minister. There were many Christians in the audience who, if they had known the truth, would have been deeply disturbed by my decision to become a Jew. What could I possibly say that would touch the heart of every individual present and still be an affirmation of my life's choice?

My mother had always taught us when we were growing up, "Whatever you do, do it with dignity." When I was young, I thought she was speaking about our own personal dignity, but, as I grew up, I came to realize she was also speaking about the dignity of others. She wanted us to carry out every deed in life with the utmost dignity and respect for the other person's position.

I would need to heed my mother's message, but I was faced with an enormous dilemma. How could I remain true to the convictions of my heart and still be sensitive to the beliefs of the people in the audience?

Those were the thoughts that careened through my mind as I looked out at the heterogeneous group. As I anxiously searched for an opening phrase, my grandmother's words reverberated in my ears: "Just ask the Lord to help you."

An announcement regarding the service shocked me back into awareness of where I was standing. I looked out at the audience and saw Ruth's eyes. She was the only person in the audience who grasped the enormity of my problem. With a tearful look, she gave me a gentle nod of approval.

I began my sermon with an affectionate description of my mother's hobby, collecting international dolls. I had my own "United Nations" of dolls in my bedroom, I told them. I felt myself grow calm. The words began to arrange themselves with little effort on my part.

"Abraham, our patriarch, was the progenitor of the three major religions," I said. "He was also the main protagonist of my life."

I shared with the audience my favorite story from the time that I had first started reading the Bible. I used to close my eyes and pretend that Abraham was my great-grandfather, and everywhere he went I was by his side, a little child holding his hand — "I walked with him through the entire Land of Israel."

I then approached the most delicate part of my talk. "Today my childhood aspiration is being realized. When I leave Switzerland, I will be returning to my new spiritual home, Israel." I told the audience of the startled and critical reaction my decision had provoked among my friends in the United States. "Please don't tell anyone that you're moving to Israel," one of my friends implored me. "They'll think you're crazy."

Everyone there broke out in laughter with me. In this, my last sermon, I had indeed reached their hearts.

I had been a successful, middle-class, African-American professional with a comfortable lifestyle in California. All my major life needs, material and spiritual alike, had been met...or so I thought. But the irresistible call of God to make Israel my home and the Jews my people was so strong that I was prepared to give up everything: home, possessions, friends, and even my family.

When people ask me what made me want to undergo the difficult and radical transformation of becoming a Jew, I tell them, "I was inspired by God's divine call to our father, Abraham." That call represented an awesome spiritual summons to Abraham and to all those who followed in his footsteps.

"*Lech lecha*," the passage begins in Hebrew, as God speaks to Abraham. "Go for yourself from your land, from your birthplace, and from your father's house, to the land that I will show you."

Only God — the great artist of the universe — could bring about the first imaginary steps in the secret thought-life of a little Black child and lead her all the way along a path which grows clearer day by day. I really don't know where I would be if not for the awesome spiritual power contained in God's call to Abraham and to all those who follow in his footsteps. A convert has to esteem God above her very own family. That became clear to me as I began to undertake the painful process of separating from everything and everyone whom I had held dear my entire life.

Lech lecha: And so I left my native land, my family, my relatives, and my father's house to go up to the Land of Israel, the land of my ancestors, the land of my soul.

Chapter 1

Grandma's Hands

The view from my first apartment in Bayit Vegan, Jerusalem, was breathtaking. To the east, I could see the new villas of Ramat Sharet and the picturesque gardens of the Holyland Hotel, and down below that the Malcha Shopping Center and the Teddy Kollek Sports Stadium. Past Malcha the road climbed steeply to the sweeping crest of Gilo, the highest in altitude of all Jerusalem's neighborhoods. Behind Gilo and further east, Bethlehem and the settlements of Gush Etzion skirted a high plateau to the southeast.

The aroma of the apple pie baking in the oven filled the room. I started to sing "Grandma's Hands," as recorded by Bill Withers.

Grandma's hands used to hand me a piece of candy.
Grandma's hands picked me up each time I fell.
Grandma's hands really came in handy,
"Nancy, why you want to spank that boy,
What do you want to spank him for,
He didn't drop no apple core."
But I don't have Grandma anymore.
When I get to Heaven I'll look for Grandma's hands.

But I don't have Grandma anymore.
When I get to Heaven I'll look for Grandma's hands.

I would always sing that song when I made apple pies. I thought that perhaps the singing might help me bake pies almost as good as Grandmother's, especially in my kosher kitchen.

I remember once watching Grandmother Gray preparing a pie for me to take home. She peeled her homegrown apples with precision, boiled them, then added about two tablespoons of butter, a teaspoon each of nutmeg and vanilla, and half a cup of sugar...and that was it! For the crust, the best part of all, she worked a little Crisco, water, and a pinch of salt into three cups of sifted flour. It was always golden brown on top, and each pie was better than the one before.

Married at a very young age, my paternal grandparents were gentle, refined, and religious folk. Sylvester and Ola C. Gray lived in Mound Bayou, Mississippi, where the entire municipality, hospitals, schools, police and fire department, town hall, houses of worship, and businesses were all owned and operated by Blacks.

Great love and mutual respect filled the Gray home. Since I was always in awe of my grandparents' spirituality, I never paid much attention to their outward appearance. Now, when I sit and look at the family album, I see the stark contrast in their looks.

Granddaddy had keen features and beautiful black skin unmarred by any wrinkles. His mother, Georgiana, and his father, Poppalee Gray, were from Vicksburg, Mississippi, and later moved to Merrigold. I remember Granddaddy telling me the family history as passed down by his elders. Poppalee's mother was a Native American. His wife Georgiana, whom we called Mama Georgia, was a Geishaw, a member of a group of Africans who traveled on slave ships to Louisiana via France, and ultimately settled in New Orleans. I can remember her beautiful pale-red skin and long black braids. Poppalee was brown-skinned and full of energy.

Grandmother was slightly taller than Granddaddy, with a kind of Southern sophistication. She had a fair complexion, which was important to Black folk in those days — White people took more kindly to the fair-skinned Negroes. Grandmother's English was impeccable, or at least I thought so. It seemed as if she was always correcting everyone's speech and behavior. "You chillun have got to learn to speak proper English if the White man is going to hire you. You must get an education." I don't ever recall a harsh word passing her lips. And yet I didn't resent her advice; instinctively, I knew what she said was for my well-being.

Grandmother's family, the McWilliams, were educated. Her brother owned an entire block of businesses in Clarkdale, Mississippi — a grocery store, cleaners, and the funeral parlor. Once, when we visited them, I remember Grandmother pointing out all the businesses with a palpable sense of pride.

During summer vacation, my older brother, Oscar, my sister, Nellie, and I, plus several cousins, were sent down South from Chicago, where we lived, to visit our grandparents on their 125-acre farm. In addition to the summer crew, we had three uncles and three aunts, all unmarried, living there. To us children, the house seemed so huge. Now I wonder how we all fit into those five small rooms, but Grandmother and Granddaddy were always glad to have all of us.

Those brief annual visits remain among my most cherished memories. I loved the beautiful blossoms, the fragrance of the fruits, the peach trees, the apple orchard that surrounded the house, and, most of all, the pecan trees. I remember also complaining forever about the pump and the toilet which, in the early years, were both outside. One year my constant worry was that my precious patent leather shoes would not survive the muddy, unpaved roads.

Their house looked like all the others in that part of the South: wood-framed, two steps up to the porch, and a screened doorway to the living room. I learned later that they were called shotgun houses: If you shot a bullet into the front door it would go straight out through the back way. In the kitchen stood an old potbellied stove from which Grandmother served her home-cooked delights. The homey table and chairs, where we all managed to fit quite nicely, were in the middle of the room. Granddaddy always relaxed in his rocking chair next to the old piano in the living room. The old wooden rocker had a pretty floral seat cushion, with a matching cover for the sofa, that Grandmother had made.

"There's boys' work and there's girls' work," Granddaddy used to say. He made sure, however, that the work was divided equally. Alas, his idea of girls' work included feeding the geese and chickens and milking the cows, as well as picking cotton. As a city girl, I was terrified of live farm animals. My feeling was that they belonged in a zoo. The chickens always seemed to be pecking at my feet from all sides and the geese were the messiest, most miserable creatures I'd ever laid eyes upon! I wondered why they made such an angry racket.

Grandma's hands picked me up each time I fell.

Even as an eight-year-old, I refused to believe that God had created me to pick cotton. In retrospect, I think that my childhood aversion to farm work arose from the perception that engaging in those activities was not my true purpose in life. I felt a deep hunger for spirituality — for some meaningful cause to which I could devote my life.

I loathed picking cotton. It was hard work, done in beastly hot weather. In my mind I can picture my aching hands covered with bandages in an attempt to protect my fingers from the sharp hulls of the cotton. I had to cross a rickety old bridge to get to the cotton fields. My biggest fear was that I would fall off that bridge into the muddy creek below. One day, of course, I did! My brother Oscar and one of my uncles jumped into the creek to rescue me. Their efforts were successful and greatly appreciated. At least I wasn't wearing my patent-leather shoes! All I remember is my screaming and thinking, *How could such a horrible thing happen to a nice girl like me?*

Grandma's hands used to hand me a piece of candy.

My brother Oscar carried me back to my grandmother, whose warm hug and embrace soon calmed my fears. She gave me my favorite lollipop and a nice warm bath. Granddaddy, responsible gentleman that he was, fixed the bridge that same day. However, I could not be persuaded to return to the cotton fields.

Nancy, why you want to spank that boy, / What do you want to spank him for, / He didn't drop no apple core.

Granddaddy was the disciplinarian. Whenever any of the grandchildren disobeyed, he'd send another outside to get his "switch." We all knew what that meant! "Now, Syl, that's enough," Grandmother would say. She was the softhearted one. "Don't you whip that child too much!" I never received a whipping. Just hearing the wails of a recipient of Granddaddy's switch was enough to keep me in line.

Grandmother possessed outstanding skills in all the domestic arts. She made some of the most beautiful patchwork quilts I've ever seen in my life. But her main teaching to her children and grandchildren was about obedience to God. Her close relationship with Him grew and flourished, nourished by her prayers and complete trust in her Creator. As Baptists, my grandparents believed very strongly in Bible study and prayer. At the dinner table my grandfather would start the prayers, and then each child, from the eldest to the youngest, had to recite a Bible verse. The only verse I could remember was "The Lord is my Shepherd," from the twenty-third Psalm. Every evening after dinner we would gather in the living room and entertain ourselves with Bible quizzes. We had no television, so our primary nighttime entertainment was to memorize all the names of the books and characters of the Bible.

Grandmother taught all her children and grandchildren the twenty-third Psalm. I couldn't have been more than four years old when she first taught it to me on one of her visits to Chicago. It tells us, she would explain, "that God provides for all mankind and He fulfills our every need." Maybe because I was so young, Grandmother's words made a deep impression that has stayed with me throughout the years. Whenever any difficulty arose, I followed my grandmother's example and "set up residence" in the Book of Psalms.

Many years later, while working for Continental Airlines, I experienced one of the most rewarding visits I'd ever had with my grandparents. Travel concessions from my employer in California made a visit possible during July, the hottest month of the year. That stay was to become a turning point in my life.

I had always felt drawn to my grandparents and wondered

what it was that pulled me so strongly to them. Over the years I gradually came to realize that it was the rare peace and stability of my grandparents' home that called to me. I realized that my grandparents had laid the foundation for the spiritual upbringing of all their children, grandchildren, and even great-grandchildren. Throughout my entire spiritual journey their lives remained a constant source of strength. Whenever any of us became ill, Grandmother, like the people of the Bible, believed that it was the Lord that would do the healing, not the doctors. Years later when I studied medical treatment during Biblical days, I discovered that the Jewish people went to the prophets when they became ill. I was also taught in seminary that sickness is often a spiritual problem that manifests itself through the physical. Today I marvel at how my grandparents, though uneducated academically, were somehow extremely knowledgeable of Biblical concepts.

But now I wasn't a little girl in patent leather shoes. I was a travel executive in my forties, on a visit to my aging grandparents. My Uncle Jesse picked me up at Greenville Airport. The sight of the lush green weeping willows that lined the paved road to Grandmother's house was so beautiful. Even the swamp that was necessary for the weeping willows' survival had a certain charm. I could hear the mosquitoes buzzing around. The air was so fresh and clean, in sharp contrast to the California smog I'd grown used to. "The earth is the Lord's, Uncle Jesse," I chanted as I fastened my seat belt.

The ride to my grandparents gave me sufficient time to catch up on family details. They had completed the building of their new home and Uncle Jesse had a job at the Baxter Pharmaceutical Company.

As we turned down the road to Grandma's I could smell the aroma of the fruit orchard. *It's picking time,* I mused. *My, how things have changed since my last visit ten years ago.* The rickety bridge and the cotton fields were no more. The creek into which I had once fallen had dried up. The chickens and geese that had once intimidated me had become my friends: with the passage of time, I had become more appreciative of God's creation. How my perception had changed! The hand pump was useless and the outhouse had been replaced with indoor facilities. No more perilous trips to the outhouse. Even the muddy roads were paved and no longer posed a hazard to my shoes.

Granddaddy peered over his glasses as I entered the doorway. "Give me a hug, Delores." Here, in the modest living room, it seemed that little had changed. Granddaddy's old rocking chair was still in the middle of the room. The old piano was now only an heirloom, having long ago struck its last chord. The old sofa was still holding firm in the corner. The kitchen, however, had undergone a face-lift and the old pot-bellied stove, which had provided warmth as well as those well-remembered apple pies, was gone. It had been replaced by a modern gas stove which proved to me, once and for all, that it was not the stove but my grandmother's culinary talents that made the food good. She had prepared a wonderful meal of fried chicken, golden brown corn bread, and collard greens. The aroma alone transported me back in time to those big family dinners.

"Grandmother, remember how Uncle Berlin used to play Negro spirituals on the piano?"

"Yes! Delores, you chilluns had such lovely voices. It was truly a gift from God."

I knew she was being kind or perhaps she didn't remember

that I couldn't carry a tune in a bucket. Oh, how I yearned to sing like the rest of them. When my aunt, Lee Esther, would sing a solo, her voice soared to the heavens; I was sure that God was listening.

Our family had its own choir. My grandmother had even taught the girls to curtsy and the boys to bow after our performance. "I remember in the old days, how the White folk would drive for miles on Sundays just to hear Black folk sing the Negro spirituals," Grandmother remarked.

Expressing gratitude was one of her trademarks: "Delores, Syl and I are so happy that you chilluns haven't forgotten about us. We're grateful to have educated grandchildren with good careers. We still pray for all our grandchildren every night."

Grandma's hands really came in handy.

Once we had prepared for bed, I happened to walk by my grandparents' room as Grandmother was praying. I stood there mesmerized, unable to believe how long she remained on her knees. Being a Baptist, she turned up the volume when she got to her family. "And Lord, help all my children, grandchildren, and great-grandchildren to serve You." How I yearned to pray like that. I had goose pimples as I listened to her pour out her soul. What a commencement to prayer!

When at last she rose to her feet, I asked in awe, "Grandmother, you still kneel down to pray?"

She placed her hand in mine, the hand of a praying woman. "Yes, Delores, that's the only way I know how to pray. I pray that you'll always remember that your help comes from God."

"Your help comes from God." Those words have been a source of strength and comfort throughout the years. The example of Grandmother, at age seventy-eight, pouring out her heart in prayer had a profound effect on my life. Intrigued and inspired by the scene I'd witnessed, one morning shortly after my return home I decided that I too would dedicate my life to prayer. I had read in the Book of Psalms, "Evening, morning, and noon, I supplicate and moan; and He has heard my voice" (Psalms 55:18). Since King David had prayed three times a day, I would do the same, and so I did!

At this point in my life I had several years of conscientious Bible study behind me, but still, something crucial was missing. Now I knew: It was prayer.

I envied Grandmother her special relationship with her Creator. How wonderful it would be to experience just one-tenth of her spiritual devotion. Determined to gain deeper insight into my grandparents' spiritual strength, I returned each year to the farm in Mound Bayou. I knew that a vital element was missing in my life, and I knew also that I wanted it far more than anything else. Having learned more about God through studying the Bible, I recognized that my grandparents were the two holiest people I had ever known.

When I told Grandmother that I was planning to become a minister, she wrote me a beautiful letter. She was delighted with the knowledge that I had decided to dedicate my life to prayer and to studying the Bible. She gave me this rule to apply to my studies: "Delores, you must study the word of God to know His will, and He will guide your life. Since you love to pray, you must pray until you get an answer. Don't get weary if He delays, you hear! God's delay does not mean no."

Years later, while browsing in a bookstore in Safed during a tour I was leading to the Holy Land, I saw a book called a "Jewish

Siddur." I had no idea at that time what a Jewish prayer book was. When I opened the book my first impression was, *These prayers are very powerful! I have to buy this book.*

I started praying from that book on the bus with my tour group from the States. I couldn't put it down. At one point I was so moved, I started crying. I was reading some of my favorite psalms, "I was a youth and also have aged, and I have not seen a righteous man forsaken, nor his children begging for bread. God will give might to His people; God will bless His people with peace" (Psalms 37:25, 29:11). I realized that everything my grandmother had spoken about and believed in could be found in the Book of Psalms. At the time I was a minister, with no idea of how Jewish people prayed. I did not even know that Jews prayed three times a day. I would just open the book and read the prayers at random. Yet my grandmother's strong ethical teachings, which she had gotten from the Psalms, were beginning to change my life.

My grandparents were privileged to celebrate their fiftieth wedding anniversary. I was honored to officiate as minister in the renewal of their wedding vows. My sister was unable to attend due to work commitments, but she contributed by making a veil for my grandmother. My grandparents were the spiritual pillars that held us together as a family. I will forever cherish the fond memories of their Godly lives. The peace that continued to draw me to their home I've found here in Bayit Vegan in the homes of my new family, the Jewish people.

After my grandfather's death in 1986, my grandmother was diagnosed with an aneurysm. Still grieving over the loss of her husband, she had lost the will to live. The doctors weren't expecting her to survive, but we didn't care what they said. We had faith in

God. Our entire family prayed and fasted. When Grandmother went back to the doctor, he couldn't find the aneurysm. It was gone! We were overjoyed to do for our grandmother what she would have done for us in the same situation. We were convinced that because of our prayers God had granted her more time to be with us.

Two years later, my family mourned the indescribable loss of my grandmother, Ola C. Gray, a woman of boundless faith. She died a natural death. I am certain that Grandma's words and deeds have earned her a share in the World to Come. She wasn't aware of the seven Noachide Laws, but she lived by them. Solomon, the King of Israel who bequeathed God's treasures of wisdom to Jew and gentile alike, wrote: "A good man leaves an inheritance to his children's children" (Proverbs 13:22). Rashi explains, "A good man will leave an inheritance of his merit and his property to his sons' sons, but a sinner does not leave over an inheritance to his sons, for his wealth and his property are laid away for the righteous."

These days, whenever I make apple pie in my kosher kitchen in Bayit Vegan, the words of "Grandma's Hands" come to my lips and ignite the memory of my beloved grandmother — but my pies don't ever come out as well as hers. When I told this story to my *rebbetzin*, she said, "Ahuvah, the reason your pies don't come out like your grandmother's, even in your kosher kitchen, is because her apples were homegrown." If "homegrown" best describes Grandmother's pies, "homegrown" best describes me, as well.

Today, at the Shabbos table with my host families, the singing of beautiful Shabbos melodies sometimes transports me to the humble table of my roots. In those days the songs we sang were old, soul-stirring hymns. It was Grandmother's practice to prepare all food for Sunday on Saturday. Sunday was strictly a religious day, set aside for acknowledging the Lord.

"You chilluns have to know that you have to honor the Lord," Grandma would say. We weren't allowed to iron, or even take a bath; the only things we were permitted to do were to wash our faces and brush our teeth. Then we would get dressed, eat breakfast, and go to the house of worship. Grandmother even combed and braided our hair on Saturday night and tied it with a scarf, to ensure that we honored God.

Years later, as we studied the halachos of Shabbos in the Neve Yerushalayim Women's College in Jerusalem, my mind wandered back to my grandmother's house on the Sabbath: almost a preparatory course for observing Shabbos. Living in Jerusalem and experiencing the combination of strict discipline and warm atmosphere in Jewish homes on Shabbos so much reminds me of the warmth and peace of my grandparents' home. All the pieces to the puzzle are finally in place: The little Black girl with pigtails who used to observe all of the do's and don'ts of her grandmother in Mississippi has finally made it home. When I sit at the Shabbos table, my eyes often fill with tears when I realize it's partially in the merit of Grandmother that I became an observant Jew. *Grandma, I love you.*

Chapter 2

The Secret of My Strength

"Hey, here!"

My mother called out the quaint Southern expression as she opened the back door and saw to her amazement that the stairs of the back porch had disappeared. She was furious to be greeted by such a sight the first thing after she had come home from work. She immediately picked up the telephone and called the lawyer who managed our property for the landlord.

"Mr. Friedman, would you please explain why there are no stairs on the back porch? Do you realize that one of my children could have been injured? I strongly suggest that you get someone out immediately to replace the stairs. If anything happens to one of my children, I will sue. Goodbye!"

Within half an hour, a work crew arrived on the scene to install temporary stairs. (Later we found out that the apartment building that we were living in was being refurbished.)

During dinner we could hear the work crew with their electric saws humming away. "Way to go, Mom! You're a genius." We all applauded. I learned a valuable lesson in the art of diplomacy from my mother that day. *Efficiency par excellence,* I thought. Many years later this story was still a source of amusement for my siblings and me.

The secret of my strength in facing the trials and challenges of my life's journey, I attribute to my mother's strength. At every turning point in my life, whether in a new country experiencing culture shock or starting a new way of life, I would always hear my mother's words, "Hey, here!" and remember how briskly and effectively she'd solved that minor household crisis.

"She arises while it is yet night, and gives food to her house-hold and a portion to her maidens" (Proverbs 31:20).

My mother rose at 4:30 A.M. five days a week to go to work. She often couldn't find her shoes in the darkness of the predawn hour. When she called out, "Where are my shoes?" I'd tumble out of bed to find them so the family shouldn't be awakened. That noble act earned me the title of "Mom's right-hand girl." On mornings that she was ill I'd say, "Mother, please don't go to work. You're not feeling well." She'd typically reply, "Don't worry, Delores, I'll be fine once I get there." When I became a working woman myself, the memory of Mother, leaning on the wall as she fumbled for the doorknob, helped me to keep going in times of illness or stress.

As a teenager I imagined that my parents must be wealthy. They were such good providers. As an adult I realized that, sick or well, they worked extremely hard and underwent great sacrifices to meet the needs of our family.

When Mother retired from her job as a machinist at National Biscuit Company — Nabisco — the management made a special lunch in her honor and bought her lovely gifts. My sister, Nellie, and I walked through the plant by her side, adorned in the striking white nautical dresses my sister had sewn.

As the hour approached for her grand finale, Mother began to weep. My sister and I were both silent. I wondered why Mother was crying. I thought about the numerous times I had come to the plant to pick her up after work. We would stroll through the plant, and I'd meet all her friends. What impressed me most about those strolls were the unusual names of her coworkers. "Pigtail, this is Delores."

Once out of hearing range, I asked, "Mother, is her name really Pigtail?"

"Yes, we grew up together in Clarkdale, Mississippi."

Further along, we met another worker. "Chris, is that Nellie?"

"No, it's Delores," Mother answered.

"Who was that, Mother?"

"Her name is Hot Tamale Mary, and she has known you since you were a baby."

The names were strange to me, but to Mother they were friends.

The sound of weeping snapped me back to the present. "Mother, why are you crying?"

Uncharacteristically, she didn't answer until several years later, during one of our frequent heart-to-heart talks. She explained her tears at that time. "Delores, I was leaving behind forty-two years of my life."

Today I cherish the accolades that were awarded to my mother at her farewell luncheon and retirement party. They expressed the love and respect of her coworkers and employers alike. She was my role model; from her example I learned the value of being a responsible human being.

She devoted her entire life to the welfare of her family and other people. I don't recall her ever taking a vacation until I was an adult. However, cost was never a consideration when she sent us on trips to visit our grandparents. Surely she realized the significance of those visits, which later transformed my life. They slowly began the planting of the seeds that eventually blossomed into an awakening to the belief of the one God.

I grew up in the Lawndale Douglas Park area, an African-American neighborhood of Chicago. We lived on the second floor of an apartment building. Our neighbors were all working-class families with children. It was a quiet area with a lovely park as well as a playground with a basketball court. I attended the Hertzl Grade School, originally established by the Jewish community. After graduation, I attended the John Marshall High School, famous for its basketball team. I became a cheerleader in my junior year and as a senior was editor of the high school newspaper. Those school years were among the most enjoyable ones of my life. I was very popular, had lots of friends, participated in spelling matches, and maintained an A-, B+ average. Even though I was the youngest, I used to help my siblings with their math and spelling homework. I can remember thinking to myself, *Who is going to help me?*

My mother and my natural father divorced when I was very young. I was three years old when Mother remarried Ezra Buckner, a fellow worker at Nabisco. Our stepfather took over the reins of the household and raised us as if he were our real father. We called him "Dad." (Our natural father we called "Daddy.") Within a few years our family began to grow. We were thrilled to have two new additions, Ezra Jr. and Lorenzo (Rennie). Dad taught us everything: how to say grace before meals, how to hold a knife and fork, how to sit up properly at the table, and how to leave graciously. "Slide your chair under the table; walk — don't run," he'd say.

There was never a dull moment in our home. My oldest brother, Oscar, was quiet and mild-tempered. My sister, Nellie, was the family spokesperson. To my parents I was the "spoiled brat," given everything I wanted. My hobbies were tap-dancing, ballet, reading, swimming, and horseback riding. We were given plenty of latitude for educational pastimes such as museums, theater, and ballets. It was Mother who always made sure that we had all the various fun foods to make our picnics successful — potato chips, apples, grapes, and drinks. She took us shopping for holiday clothes — pink for Nellie and blue for me. Though pink was Mother's favorite color, she always insisted that I looked better in blue. In my adult years I had half of my wardrobe in pink — in protest!

Dad would take us fishing with him periodically. I vividly recall one time when he allowed my brother Ezra and me to go hunting with him and some colleagues. The rabbits were running through the fields and pheasants were flying through the air. I thought I was watching a Walt Disney movie.

The atmosphere in our home was warm and comfortable. At dinner, Dad would ask each of us, "How was your day at school?" Mom would add, "Are you accomplishing your study goals?" Often the conversation turned to what we wanted to be when we grew up.

More than once Oscar exclaimed, "I want to be a policeman." Indeed, he became a deputy sheriff. Nellie always said, "I would like to be an artist." She later became a graphic artist. The seeds of our future were planted and nurtured at that table.

My reply always aroused laughter. "I want to be like Princess Grace of Monaco."

"Why?" Dad asked.

"Because I think she's charming and beautiful!" I exclaimed. In reality, I couldn't think of anything else I wanted to be at that time. I felt I had plenty of time to decide.

After dinner I'd often go off to the bathroom and practice my tap-dancing: Shuffle, shuffle, slide, shuffle shuffle, time step, slide, until Oscar would beg me to stop.

Holidays with my parents were so lovely! My parents would buy gifts for all their children and grandchildren and favorite dishes would be prepared for all. Thanksgiving was a festive array of good food, fun, and laughter. My mother and Nellie did most of the cooking. When the two of them were in the kitchen, I would vacate the premises because I simply couldn't keep up with the pace!

As time passed I started becoming more responsible. By the time I was in eighth grade, I decided I wanted a job. I was keen on competing with my younger brother, Ezra Jr., who was already delivering papers. By that time, my family had moved and bought a two-flat building on West Polk Street. Each day I would take the long route home from school just to pass by Jaynette's, a beautiful dress shop on Pulaski Road. One day I squared my shoulders, walked in, and said, "Hello, my name is Delores Gray. I am looking for a job. Do you need help?"

They looked at me and then at each other and said in unison, "Can you start now?"

Without hesitation I replied, "Yes."

Proudly, I told my parents about my accomplishment. Nellie

said it was my smile that got me the job, and we all laughed.

I felt completely at home with the owners of the dress shop, Mr. and Mrs. Greenberg and Mrs. G.'s sister Jeanette. They were in their early sixties, each endowed with an irrepressible Jewish sense of humor, all the more entertaining because of their Southern Jewish accent. My parents grew up in the South, and I've always felt at home in the company of Southerners.

After a short period of working for the Greenbergs, I learned how to trim the window. One day Mrs. Greenberg asked me if I was willing to go to the merchandise mart with her to buy clothing for the store. She said my charming smile would help. *Oh, Nellie, how right you were!*

I continued working at Jaynette's Dress Shop throughout high school. The Greenbergs were the first contact I had with a Jewish family, and we became very close. Before long, they started inviting me home with them for the weekends. On Friday nights, they would light candles and serve gefilte fish, chicken soup, and matzah balls, the traditional Friday night meal. We also had wine and "challah," a special, good-tasting bread. Our Friday nights were very warm and wholesome; it was just like being with my own family. But I never told my mother we had wine. She would have *"plotzed"* – she herself never took a drop of liquor in her life!

Mrs. G. used to give me lovely presents for my birthday, graduation, and the holiday season. On one memorable occasion I was given the privilege to select whatever I wanted in the store. Jeanette said, "Mrs. G., you know Delores has good taste." I chose a smashing royal blue pullover and cardigan sweater set for myself.

Every week, I took home gifts for Mother and clothing for my sister and myself. As a result, I hardly managed to keep any of my salary. Mother soon became known as one of the best-dressed women in the neighborhood. One day I took my paycheck and bought her a pair of very expensive boots. She wept when she saw them. Bewildered, I asked, "Mother, don't you like your new boots?"

"Delores, this is the first pair I've ever had, and they're gorgeous." With that, we both began crying, but they were tears of joy.

Mother often told me that I should save my money and not spend so much. I knew she was right. One Friday, as I was leaving work for the weekend, Mrs. G. said, "Delores, aren't you going to bring your mother a gift?"

"No," I said. "I am going to save my paycheck this week and open a bank account."

Mrs. G. went to the sweater counter, took out a cardigan in my mother's size, and said, "Here, Delores, give this to your mother and don't tell her it's from us."

That was when I learned one of the basic Jewish tenets of giving charity — to give anonymously. The love and generosity in this gesture touched me deeply. I gave Mrs. G. and Jeanette each a big hug laced with tears; we were a teary-eyed threesome.

There were numerous times when the Greenbergs showered us with gifts. When I bought my mother a suit for her birthday, they donated the necklace. When I bought a dress for my sister, they chipped in a scarf.

Our families loved each other. Occasionally, my mother and sister visited the dress shop. Mrs. G. made each of their visits an occasion, serving tea and cookies or lox and bagels with cream cheese to enhance our cozy chat.

Afterwards, Mrs. G. would say with her Southern twang,

"De-lores, your mother is such a beautiful woman. One day, you'll look just like her."

I would think to myself, *Not in this lifetime – it's impossible.* My mother and sister were gorgeous, whereas I was just ordinary looking!

I had never thought of myself as attractive. Despite my modesty, I was finally persuaded to run for Homecoming Queen and participate in beauty pageants. Because I never gave the pageants my full efforts, I was always placed second or runner-up. But truth told, I really didn't mind missing out on first place; I didn't want to be known as just a pretty face and felt very uncomfortable being a public spectacle. Later, as an Orthodox Jew, I learned that modesty is a prerequisite and honorable trait for every human being.

My eldest brother, Oscar, was always very protective of my sister and me; in fact, Nellie and I were known in the neighborhood as "Oscar's sisters"! When we were growing up, all of his male friends were forewarned before they visited our home, "I've got two sisters, and they are off-limits to you. You can say hello, but don't engage in any lengthy conversations." Once I overheard him saying it and was genuinely impressed by Oscar's candid love and concern for us.

Though there was a strong street gang presence in our neighborhood, Oscar never became involved. The first and only time a gang approached him to entice him to join them, he went straight to my parents. My parents, who never missed a beat when it came to taking care of their children, quickly dispatched Oscar to our grandparents in Mississippi, where he finished high school.

Time passed and Oscar was drafted into the army. The United States was fighting in Vietnam. The song "You're in the

Army Now" was popular. Every time I heard it, I would think about my brother and start crying. That led me to start praying. My prayer began with, "Dear God, I pray to the God of Abraham, Isaac, and Jacob. Please don't send my brother to Vietnam." Though I had been taught to preface every prayer "Our Father in Heaven," I felt the need to pray to the God of Abraham, Isaac, and Jacob, whom I had read about in the Bible. The God of the three great patriarchs answered my prayers: instead of going to Vietnam, my brother was sent to Germany for two years! That was when I began to realize the benefit of prayer. (When Oscar returned he married Dorothy Johnson, his childhood companion. Their daughter Debra is my oldest niece.)

My mother had a marvelous way of explaining my brother Ezra's personality: "Don't worry. He's just an active child." One of his favorite tricks was to go to Sears & Roebuck instead of coming home and sit in their electronics department watching television till late in the evening. Poor Mother would be leaning out the window calling his name. But Mom was right in not worrying about Ezra. Within a few years he outgrew his reputation in the neighborhood for being mischievous. He soon dropped his paper route and started earning a hefty salary at an Italian beef stand. Little did I know in those days that in years to come this brother would test my faith, on the day when I would be led to the gates of prayer with his life hanging on the line!

The rules in the house were that you went to school, graduated, got a job, and then married. After Nellie's high school graduation she married her childhood sweetheart Andrew Prestwood, who had joined the Air Force. Later they moved to Bermuda.

Even though my mother had only finished grade school, she always stressed the importance of an education. She went to great sacrifice to ensure that we all studied at college. At her behest I was shipped off to Eastern Illinois University in Charleston, Illinois, on a four-year scholarship. During my summer vacations I continued to work for the Greenbergs.

I left college after two years and began working with the First National Bank of Chicago. After a few years there, I was encouraged to apply for a job with Continental Airlines as a stewardess. Within ten days I was on my way to be interviewed for a position, flying in an airplane for the first time in my life. I didn't tell anyone that I was going.

The airport in Los Angeles resembled all the airport scenes I had seen in the movies. I took a cab to Continental's corporate office. After responding candidly to the interviewer's questions and having my height and weight measured, I was told that I had been hired. I was to report back within two weeks to begin six weeks of training.

On my return flight to Chicago that evening, I was glowing; I felt a strong sense of accomplishment. I thought to myself, *That's not bad for a twenty-three-year-old Black woman!* James Brown had a hit at the time, "Say It Loud — I Am Black and I Am Proud," which perfectly captured my feelings.

Back on the ground and headed for home, my thoughts shifted to my parents. I pictured how proud they would be. When I realized it would be midnight before I got in, I knew they would also be very worried. Mother and Dad were still up in the living room when I opened the door.

"Where have you been?" Mother asked, visibly relieved.

"You may not believe this," I said, beaming, "but I have just come back from Los Angeles. I was hired by Continental Airlines as a stewardess." My parents were as elated as I was, even though my new career would take me far from home.

Thus began the start of a twenty-three-year career with Continental. As a flight attendant, I flew turnaround flights from Chicago to Los Angeles in a combination of lights, camera, and action. I constantly scurried from one "scene" to another, living out of a suitcase. I had two pairs of electric curlers and two complete makeup kits, one for home and one for the road.

My new job required that I move to California. How I cherished my thrice-annual visits home! Every time I stepped into my bedroom I took a journey back through time. I felt like a princess returning to her castle. Mother always prepared everything; the dolls were all in place over my bed — all fifty of them!

Each time I came home, the "family" seemed to have increased. There was a native American doll, a Dutch doll, a Japanese doll, a Black doll, and more. I don't know what motivated my mother to start collecting dolls, but when she retired it became her hobby.

I would hurry through the unpacking so I could join Mother in the kitchen. She always prepared my favorite welcome-home meal: fried chicken, collard greens, sweet potatoes, and corn bread, with peach cobbler for dessert.

Following dinner, Mother and I retreated to our favorite spot, her bedroom, to dive deeply into family memories. "Do you remember the time when I fell off that bridge in Mississippi?"

Our laughter reverberated throughout the house. Without fail, in exactly two minutes, Dad, who was cleaning up and slaving away in the kitchen, was standing in the doorway laughing with us.

"What are you two laughing about?"

I finally composed myself enough to say, "The time when I

fell off that old raggedy bridge at Grandmother's. Remember when you heard about it, you decided not to send me back to Grandmother until I was a teenager? Whenever I hear the old Negro spiritual 'Oh, Jordan River, It's So Chilly and Cold,' I picture that muddy ditch and the crude bridge. I am so glad you didn't send me back until I grew up."

Together with those shared moments of laughter, I remember my mother's acts of kindness to strangers. When my parents purchased a duplex, we also acquired two elderly men who had lived with the previous owner. My mother asked what would happen to them once we took possession. When they were told that Jimmy, an Italian, and John, a Swede, would have to go to a nursing home, my parents allowed them to stay with us instead. Moreover, Mother looked after them until they left this world. They became a part of our family. On another occasion, Deacon Hill, a member of our place of worship, became very ill with cancer. My parents took him in and cared for the dying man until his demise.

"She spreads out her palm to the poor, and extends her hand to the destitute" (Proverbs 31:20).

We often had numerous guests in our home for dinner. Among them would be the skid-row bums who'd wandered into our neighborhood. My mother took them in from off the street. They were ushered into our bathroom to wash up and then invited to join us for dinner. Afterwards, Mother would give our guests (as she called them) food and a clean set of clothing to take with them.

Thus it was no surprise that when Dad's sister, Aunt Catherine, was dying of cancer, she moved in. She too was taken care of until her passing.

I myself was once the recipient of my parents' loving-kindness to the sick. I had gone into a state of deep depression, and my mother took me to our family doctor. All I remember is that I was almost comatose. I had to take a pill to get up and a pill to lie down. Oh, how I wished I could remember just one verse from the Bible! My parents lovingly brought all my meals to the bedroom, where my mother had to feed me. This went on for several days. One day when my mother was leaving my room she broke down in tears and sighed, "Lord, help my child to recover."

When I heard her sobbing, I made a decision to get out of that bed. Slowly my memory of the Bible came back. At first the only verse I could remember was from Isaiah. "He gives power to the faint" (Isaiah 40:29).

Months later, when my mother and I were discussing the incident, she related the following story:

"Delores, I was very worried about you, and I didn't know what to do. One day I went to work and talked to God all day. 'Lord, You know I've cared for all these sick people over the years. Now my child is very ill, and I know You can heal her.'

"Later on that day at work, a song came into my heart and I just started singing. The song was, 'They that wait on the Lord shall renew their strength. They shall mount up on wings as eagles. They shall run and not be weary; they shall walk and not faint' (Isaiah 40:31).

"When I came home that evening, I went directly to your room and heard you saying, 'He gives power to the faint.' I knew then that God had heard my prayers. I knew then that I didn't have to worry, because your love for the word of God had come back. My prayers had been answered.

"Delores, it's no secret that God is going to do something

very special in your life."

Hearing her words, I finally understood the Black idiom, "There is no secret to what God can do."

For me viewing the impressive portrait of the woman of valor of King Solomon's Proverbs (chapter 31) is like peering at old photos of my mother in our family album — so accurate is the picture that it portrays of my mother's noble qualities. Throughout her entire life my mother dedicated herself to bringing comfort and joy to others. Most of all, she did it with joy!

She must have known intuitively what I was later to learn in my seminary in Jerusalem, that a good deed done with a joyful heart has more merit in the World to Come.

My mother always loved it when I, her preaching daughter, quoted psalms, especially her favorite, Psalm 27. Just as that psalm gave strength to my mother, it strengthens me today. Many a time, when I encounter the challenges of life, I turn to it. My favorite verse is the tenth: "For even if my father and mother would have forsaken me, God would still take me up."

Mother, you are the secret of my strength to this day. In the Jewish tradition, the highest form of help we can give to a person in need is the resources that will enable him to provide for himself and others. That epitomizes what you have given me. Today, thanks to your priceless legacy, I am able to go from strength to strength. When the Creator apportioned my family legacy, He truly granted me a wonderful gift.

Chapter 3

Journey of Faith

Like most mothers, mine worried about her remaining single daughter. She was eager to marry me off. About the time I embarked on my new career, Mother embarked on her "blind-date campaign." It was so embarrassing! Most of the men were sons of her coworkers at Nabisco, and I had nothing in common with any of them. On such dates I made sure my behavior would make it impossible for any of them to call again!

One day she said in a carefully offhanded way, "You know who I just met at the supermarket? Remember Henry Simmons?"

My guard went up immediately. "You mean the Henry Simmons who used to be at our house every day, the one you always had to send home every evening?"

"That's the one," she replied.

From that point on, it was a done deal.

Thanks to Mother's diligence, Henry and I were set up on a date. We went out together every available night for a full month. We felt a strong commitment and married two months later.

A single woman no longer, I applied for a position with Continental Airlines that required less travel and would keep me closer to home. I was accepted as a flight-attendant supervisor and five years later was promoted to Sales and Marketing. Henry and I worked, saved our money, and bought our first home before our third wedding anniversary. Two years later we bought a duplex building and continued to prosper.

As time passed I developed a personal program of regular Bible study. Reading the Bible, not infrequently all through the night without sleeping, had become a routine in my life; eventually it took up most of my spare time. I would even miss social engagements rather than forfeit my treasured Bible study.

I became increasingly more dedicated to my place of worship and my commitment to God. For eight years I served as an active member of King David in Chicago.

Whenever I wanted to verify the Christian ideologies and philosophies, I'd refer to the Tanach as an authoritative cross-reference. As a Christian I felt that I couldn't possibly understand my own religion, which had evolved from Judaism, unless I understood the Torah and the history of God's Chosen People. I wanted to know how my spiritual ancestors had prayed, how they had worshiped, and how they had lived.

Regretfully, with the passing of time my personal path diverged from that of my husband's. Sadly but amicably, Henry and I divorced. We had been married for sixteen years, and had no children.

At about the same time, Continental Airlines transferred me to Los Angeles. I packed up and moved to a beautiful condominium in the San Fernando Valley, a perfect location. Even though I had a wonderful place to live, I also felt compelled to find a spiritual home. Nellie, who had become a well-established graphic artist, lived in Beverly Hills. I knew she would assist me on my journey of faith.

One day, while we were having lunch, Valerie Williamson, a friend of Nellie's, stopped by. Upon hearing of my quest, Valerie's face lit up. "Do I have the right place for you!" she exclaimed. "It's called Strait-Way. The spiritual leader is extremely erudite. He actually teaches the Jewish text in the original Hebrew."

"Really?" I exclaimed. "I've been yearning to learn Hebrew. Please take me to your leader."

The following Sunday morning after services, Valerie introduced me to Dr. Charles C. Queen. Almost without thinking, I asked if he had been to Israel. When he answered "Yes," I could hardly contain my joy. I knew in my heart that one of my prayers had been answered. A pastor right here in Los Angeles who had been to Israel, who knew Hebrew — and who had a lovely wife as well!

"It's a pleasure to meet you, Pastor Queen," I managed to say.

I became a member of Strait-Way on my second visit and almost immediately developed a close relationship with Dr. Queen and his wife, Phyllis. They graciously accepted my phone calls, no matter what time of day or night. "It's Delores," Mrs. Queen would say. "She has another question."

Thank God, I had finally found someone who could answer my questions satisfactorily. "Yes, daughter, what can I help you with?" Pastor Queen would say with unwavering patience. He always took the necessary time to thoroughly satisfy my queries, and we had many deep philosophical conversations about religion.

One Sunday, Dr. Queen related a story from his days in boot camp in North Carolina which made a deep impression on me:

He and his army buddy, Walter, had to dig a trench at the end of a long day. They were exhausted, so they dug the trench hurriedly to finish as fast as possible. A heavy rain began in the middle of the night, and because they had not dug the trench adequately, the buddies had to get up and redo the job properly in the freezing North Carolina rain.

Many years later, this story inspired me on my path to becoming Jewish. Every obstacle I came across I considered a trench that I had not dug properly. There were times when I could vividly picture Dr. Queen and Walter in the freezing North Carolina rain. Surely if God gave them the stamina to persevere, He would do the same for me.

Dr. Queen felt the same love and affinity for the Jewish people that I did. Once, when I was sitting in his office, he told me, with tears in his eyes, "Delores, it was a journey of faith for me to renounce the Christian teachings and believe in the Oneness of God. I took this leap of faith after many years of studying the Hebrew text. It took courage for me to leave the religious organization that I was a part of for thirty years, but I don't regret my decision. I have a compulsion to connect to the Jewish people and to know the history of my spiritual roots.

"Delores, you need to study every opportunity you get. You must learn Hebrew. If you don't know the Hebrew text, it's impossible to understand the Bible."

Later, when I told my rabbi's wife in Bayit Vegan about that extraordinary pastor, she exclaimed, "Did that man realize that he was preparing you for Judaism?"

Inspired by Dr. Queen's words, I became a student of the Total Word Concept Institute, the school where he taught Hebrew. Once I completed the required studies I served as a minister, foolishly thinking that I had satisfied my spiritual quest. I struggled to find the balance between my commitment to God as a minister and my commitment to work with the airline. As much as I loved my job, I was nevertheless drawn to the spiritual side of things. During the week I would drive to work with my Bible in the car and take lunch break in my car, spending a few precious moments in the Book of Psalms. "This," I'd sigh as I opened the Bible, "is the real world."

There were over three hundred travel agencies and corporate accounts in the San Fernando Valley. My responsibility was to personally visit the one hundred top revenue producing accounts. I tried to visit every agency at least once a year.

The Valley was predominately Jewish. One Tuesday in early 1988 I called on Lenny and Mimi Rich, owners of ACT Travel. They were down-to-earth folks, and we hit it off right away. I added them to my sales calling pattern, even though they fell outside the guidelines of my revenue-producing quota. I always recommended them to corporate accounts and consequently their agency flourished and eventually became one of my top accounts.

In California, everyone makes friends. My relationship with Lenny and Mimi blossomed and began to resemble the closeness I felt with my parents and grandparents. They looked upon me as a daughter, and I called them my "Jewish parents." Lenny and Mimi were traditional Jews who kindled in me an affinity for all things Jewish. They invited me to their home for Shabbos and I spent my first Pesach (Passover) with them. I'll always cherish that first seder. When Lenny read from the Haggadah, "We were slaves to Pharaoh in Egypt," I wept. I felt as though I was connecting to some deep spiritual odyssey of the past.

When my parents visited California, I arranged for them to meet Lenny and Mimi. Pure elation swept over me as I sat with my parents, my sister, and my "Jewish family" at our favorite Chinese restaurant.

During dinner, Lenny told my family his motto: "Plan your work and work your plan." He explained to his captive audience the plan he saw for me. "I've been encouraging Delores to go to Israel and then start her own travel agency specializing in tours to the Holy Land. With her connections all over America and beyond, she'd be successful in the African American market, which is virtually untapped."

"I think it's an excellent idea," Nellie said. My parents listened quietly.

In June 1989, I was airborne for Israel. As I caught my first glimpse of the beautiful shoreline of Tel Aviv I remembered Lenny's words, "You can't sell it until you've been there, Delores. Everyone has a secret passion, something he wants to do from deep down in his heart. Just a few find a way to actualize their dreams."

When I landed at Ben Gurion Airport in Tel Aviv, I was still uneasy about my venturing on such an emotional trip. But the potential that Lenny spoke of, and his strong persistence, had brought me to see Israel with my own eyes.

My itinerary had been planned by Lenny, and the next day I joined a tour with a Catholic group. I was mesmerized by the beautiful scenery. As our van rounded the final curve before Jerusalem, my heart started pulsating as if it were coming out of my chest, and I said, "Oh my God, I am at home."

At that moment, I realized that one day I would live in Jerusalem. At last my soul had found its resting place. I caught my breath and started to sing, "Jerusalem, Jerusalem, lift up your voice and sing."

Impulsively, I turned to the woman sitting next to me and said, "I know you won't believe this, but I am going to live here one day." She nodded with a polite smile, but I saw by the look on her face that she thought I was crazy.

On the airplane returning to Los Angeles, I was so excited I couldn't sleep. All I could think about was telling my "Jewish father" that he was right. I did catch a catnap or two and each time my mind wandered back to my childhood vision in which I walked hand in hand in Israel with our father, Abraham.

I arrived home jet-lagged and decided to wait until the next morning to phone Mimi and Lenny.

After my morning prayer, I called Mimi. I noticed something unusual in her voice, but I nevertheless launched into a lengthy description of my trip. When I finished, I asked to speak to Lenny.

"Delores, are you sitting down?" Mimi asked with a strange tone in her voice. I said I was, and she told me, "Lenny is dead."

I could not believe what I had just heard. Speaking with difficulty, I asked, "How could this be? What happened? When?"

"Yesterday morning after breakfast, I went to our room and found him dead," Mimi said flatly.

"When is the funeral?"

"Today." Mimi gave me the necessary information.

I hung up and tried to prepare myself to say goodbye to Lenny Rich. I was deeply grieved by the fact that we would not be able to share all the exciting details of my wonderful trip to Israel, the trip that he had made possible.

That was my first Jewish funeral. I sat very quietly, my heart aching, listening to the eulogies. In my opinion, half had not been told. Never had I met a man who loved his family and all mankind so much. Lenny spoke little about God, but he had a deep reverence for Him. I started to reminisce. Lenny never allowed me to pay for our lunches, even though I had an expense account. When I was shopping for a new car, he went with me, marching straight into the office of the dealership owner to get me the best deal. When I listed my condominium for sale, Lenny said, "Delores, this is California, not a small town in Mississippi. You can't have strangers coming into your home when you're alone. Whenever you have a prospective buyer, you call me. If need be, Mimi and I will come over, straight away."

Returning home from the cemetery, I went immediately to the Book of Psalms. At that moment I realized that Lenny's death would have a profound effect on my life and would prove to be a turning point. Wherever his final resting place was, I wanted to be there when I had to meet my Creator.

Years later, when I shared this story in Bayit Vegan, I was told that I was echoing the words of Ruth, a true convert who had told her Jewish mother-in-law, Naomi: "Where you die, I will die, and there I will be buried" (Ruth 1:16–17).

The next morning, with Lenny's voice speaking inside my head, I asked Nellie to design a logo for DG Travel, my own travel service. For marketing purposes my new business would specialize in tours to Israel, Egypt, and Greece, targeting the African-American community. In the marketing world, such a specific focus is called niche marketing. Within two weeks the business name had been certified, and I had opened a commercial checking account and incorporated my travel agency. In thirty days I had arranged my first "Pastor's Study Tour" to Israel, headed by Dr. Charles Queen.

I continued to execute my responsibilities at Continental. It was exhausting, but I maintained both jobs for three years, until DG Travel was secure enough for me to take early retirement from the airline. I seized upon every opportunity and excuse to come to Israel, logging fourteen trips in five years. The fifteenth was the beginning of a new chapter in my life.

During that time my family thought I had fallen off the turnip truck, as Grandmother would have said. I wasn't sure myself what was happening, and no wonder. I had stopped attending services on Sundays, and no longer observed any of the major Christian holidays. Bewildered, Nellie would call me every Sunday, asking, "How can you be a minister and not go to service?"

"That's a good question, Nellie. I'd have to say you're right to ask it, but I am going through a transition, and until I can figure all this out it's best for me to study my Bible and pray at home."

How could I explain to my family the logic behind my actions? Nobody knew the discomfort I felt. I simply couldn't connect with the liturgies or the sermons. The last time I attended a Christian service I was with a friend at her place of worship. I heard the pastor say that the Jewish people had to accept the new Messiah. If not, they were all damned and going to hell. The congregation applauded approvingly.

Stunned, I got up and walked outside. I thought to myself, *Are all these people crazy? How could God forsake the Jewish people? They're His chosen people.* My heart was so grieved by his words. I couldn't describe the pain I felt. I knew that would be my last day sitting in the pews. How could Nellie or anyone else understand all that?

The most difficult part was resigning from all my responsibilities at Strait-Way. My spiritual parents, the Queens, were bereft, and so was I. How could I explain this obsession? The hours of browsing through bookstores and my telescopic vision for any book on Judaism; the schlepping back and forth across two continents.

How could I justify the anguish I caused my mother? I can still hear her words each time I called home from the airport before a trip: "Delores, you can't go back over there; they're shooting again."

Weary from pleading, she would hand the phone to my Dad so that he could talk some sense into me. "Delores, please call us as soon as you get there and as soon as you get back. We'll be praying as usual."

"Thanks for being so understanding, Dad."

Before I hung up the receiver, I could hear my mother asking in agony, "Lord, what is wrong with my child? She was one of my most obedient children. What's going on with my baby?" (Typical: I was forty-eight years old, with two younger brothers, and she still called me her "baby.")

My prayer was that I should be able to resolve the tug-of-war that was being waged inside me: Judaism verses Christianity. I hated causing my parents to worry, but I had to see where my journey of faith was leading me. I was causing undue pain and anguish to so many people. I would surely need God's help.

After moving to Los Angeles, I still traveled to Chicago to visit Mother and Dad on Mother's Day, Thanksgiving, and the holiday season. For weeks before my visit on Mother's Day 1990, I struggled to find a way to tell them that I wouldn't be home for the holiday season that year. I knew they would explode. But I could no longer keep their holidays with genuine conviction.

What if I just say that I'm coming home for her birthday? Then,

later on, I can break the news gently that I won't be home for the reli-
gious holidays. Ah, brilliant! Those were my thoughts as the landing gear was being lowered and the final descent offered us the
breathtaking view of the Chicago skyline. I could see the John
Hancock Building and the Sears Tower.

"Home sweet home," I sighed as I buckled my seat belt for
the landing. Lake Michigan seemed calm. The March winds had
long subsided.

At the baggage claim, I kept an eye out for my baby brother,
Rennie. He was a noble character, always punctual. Just as my
bags appeared, his car pulled up to the curb. My sister-in-law,
Eileen, was holding their baby Shaina, whom I was seeing for the
first time.

We were soon at my parents' home, and Mother and Dad answered the door within seconds of my ringing the bell. Familiar,
beloved aromas found their way from the kitchen to the front
door. My visit went so quickly. Several days later my parents
drove me back to the airport. Leaving them was always difficult.
When I had left to move to California, Dad cried uncontrollably.
Now he was sad as my visit drew to an end, but at last his tears
subsided. Mother managed to control hers, too.

As we embraced at the check-in counter, I told them both
how I appreciated their forbearance during my transition.

"We understand, Delores. You have to do God's will. Are you
still praying three times a day and reading your Bible?" Mom
asked.

"Yes, Mother."

"All right, Chris, you're going to make that child miss her
flight," Dad cautioned her. "Just keep studying God's Word. Remember my motto: If you get stuck on a verse and don't under-

stand, stay with it and don't go any further until you get an understanding. We'll be praying for you, Delores."

Then he began his famous parting words, and I joined him with a grin. "Call us as soon as you get home."

Aboard the plane, I thanked the Lord for blessing me with such wonderful parents. They were so true to their words. They had raised us to seek our hearts' desires and taught us that we could do anything with the help of the Almighty. Even though they weren't thrilled by the news of my not coming home for the holiday season, they respected my decision.

My parents,
Christine and
Sylvester Gray

Myself at age two

My paternal grandmother, Ola C. Gray

My mother's parents, Lelar and Willie Franklin, at the wedding of their son. *First row, right to left:* Willie and Lelar, Joe Lewis and Irma Franklin, and Irma's parents

My maternal grandparents with their son Joe (right)

My mother and her three sisters. *Left to right:* Aunt Josephine, Aunt Lillie Bee, Mother, Aunt Ernestine

My step-father, Ezra Buckner

My biological father and three siblings. *Left to right:* Ezra, Nellie, Daddy, me, and Oscar

My ex-husband, Henry, and I

My sister, Nellie

My brother Ezra, a cousin, and Ezra's wife Paula

My father's parents, Ola C. and Sylvester Gray, at their fiftieth wedding anniversary

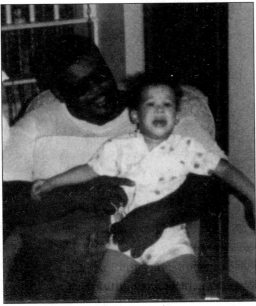

My brother Rennie with his daughter, Shaina

My niece and
nephews, then
and now:
Isaiah, Shaina,
and Leonard

Ruth
Broyde-Sharon

Leora, Ruth's daughter

Ruth's son, Alex, at his bar mitzvah

Ruth and I at a going-away party in Los Angeles

At Ruth's house on *erev Shabbos*, Culiver City, CA. *Left to right*: Ruth, Juanita Parker Scott, Wilda Spalding, Dove Geller, me, and Nellie

With a friend after a lecture in the Jewish Learning Exchange in Los Angeles, March 2000

Touring Masada with Batya Ruth Shultz

Left to right: Me, Ruthie Ingber, and Sarah Shapiro (author of *Growing with My Children*)

At a *sheva berachos* with former Neve students and close friends. Left to right: Me, Ada Sefton-Apfelbaum, Stephanie Rosenberg, Rachel Kaplan, and Faigie Langsam

At a restaurant in Jerusalem with Dovid and Pnina Shichor (who does the ticketing for my tour groups), me, and Elaine Asa (who works for Pnina's company, Bound to Travel, in Fullerton, CA)

At Stephanie Rosenberg's *vort. Left to right:* Me, Ruth Lynn, Debbie Winter, Faigie Langsam, Stephanie Rosenberg, and Stacey Katz

In New York
on a lecture
tour, October,
2000. *Left to
right*: Adam
and Pnina
Jacobs, me,
and Stacey
Katz (a friend
from Neve
Yerushalayim)

Rabbi Yosef
Ben Shlomo
Hakohen

A family collage.
First row,
left to right:
Leonard, Isaiah,
Shaina, me.
Second row:
Oscar, Rennie,
Ezra, Mother,
Dad, Nellie.

Chapter 4

Two Women, One Journey

D ivine providence is the only explanation I have for the circumstances that brought me together with Ruth Broyde-Sharon, a Jewish documentary filmmaker who became a close friend and, through our community work together, a catalyst for my conversion. I am no longer involved in the project that we worked on together before my conversion, but that project served as a stepping-stone on my journey to a full acceptance of the Covenant of Torah.

It all began in the spring of 1992. My pastor, Dr. Queen of Strait-Way in South Central Los Angeles, was planning a Passover seder for six hundred African-Americans from various parts of the city. For many of them it would be their first experience in marking the ritual feast celebrated by Jews each spring. Dr. Queen had been leading seders for our congregation for several years. He was deeply committed to teaching us about Judaism, Jewish holidays, and Jewish symbols because he felt we could not be good Christians unless we understood our spiritual roots.

I had been selected to read one of the Hebrew prayers for the seder. That night Ruth Broyde-Sharon showed up with a film crew to document the event. Later I found out that while visiting her local library she overheard two people from my place of worship request a video on the *afikoman*.

Ruth couldn't help herself. "I see you are interested in the holiday of Passover. Are you Jewish?" she asked them.

"No," they replied, "but our leader, Pastor Queen, celebrates Passover with us every year."

"Take me to your leader," Ruth said, without missing a beat.

Pastor Queen readily consented to Ruth's request to film the 1992 Passover seder, held at the Proud Bird Restaurant in Los Angeles. Several weeks later she asked to film our service on Sunday morning. She and her crew arrived and filmed highlights of our service. I could tell she was especially excited by our rhythm and blues version of the Passover song "*Dayeinu*." Pastor Queen told us that Ruth had been filming many seders around the city because she was documenting a new phenomenon, the growing number of non-Jews who were interested in celebrating Passover. She had filmed seders in a Methodist House of Worship, in Chino Men's Prison, at the Los Angeles Catholic Workers center, and many other places. At the conclusion of the service, Pastor Queen invited Ruth to the podium and gave her a special blessing for her "work of conciliation." Then he invited her to speak to the congregation.

It was unusual for a White Jewish woman to appear at a Black house of worship in Watts. We were all intrigued by her presence.

"I have a dream," she declared, echoing the famous words of the late Reverend Martin Luther King Jr. when he spoke to an overflowing crowd of civil rights activists in Washington, D.C.

"Tell it, sister," the congregation shouted excitedly. I listened spellbound. Her vision of peace and harmony among people seemed very similar to Dr. King's. When the service concluded, I went up to Ruth and introduced myself.

"Hello, Ruth. I am Delores Gray. When are you leaving for Egypt and Israel, and how many people do you have? I want to be with you on that journey."

Ruth was taken aback by my questions. "What journey? That was just a vision," she said.

"Well, if you want to take people in March, you'd better get moving," I insisted.

Ruth seemed puzzled by my comment. We conversed briefly and exchanged telephone numbers.

I called Ruth every week for two months. "How many people do you see coming from New York? How many from Philadelphia?" Finally, in an effort to end my incessant questioning, Ruth invited me to join her, her husband, Isaac, and their two children, Alex and Leora, for a Friday night Sabbath dinner.

After our Sabbath dinner Ruth said, "Okay, Delores, you keep asking me when we're going to go. So let's do it! Let's create a pilgrimage, from Egypt to Israel. Let's concentrate on bringing African-Americans and Jews together, because we have some serious repair work to do. Our two communities used to be so close, and now there is a great chasm between us. It's tragic because who better than African-Americans understand Jews and our history of persecution?"

"And who better than Jews understand African-Americans and what we went through as a people?" I replied. "Your Exodus story is also our Exodus story."

Ruth and I looked at each other, awestruck. We realized at exactly the same moment that it was nothing less than Divine providence that we had met.

As she came to know me better, Ruth was thrilled to hear

how much I loved Judaism and how I could quote Scripture. She felt that I would make an incredible ambassador to the Christian community for Judaism. "Better than another Jew," she explained, "because it will be perceived differently when a Christian speaks about Judaism in such a positive way."

We continued to meet and plan until, at last, we created the Festival of Freedom which would bring people of different cultures together for friendship and understanding.

The brochure described how we would honor Passover in its original historical setting, by beginning our journey in Egypt, traveling through the Sinai desert, and "retracing the path of the original Exodus in the footsteps of Moses, Aaron, and Miriam" to the traditional site of Mount Sinai. We would share personal stories of liberation and, as a culminating event, join together with peoples of many countries to celebrate a Universal Freedom Seder in Jerusalem.

We decided that Ruth would be the executive director and I would be the tour director because of my background in travel and marketing. We agreed that we needed to go on a pilot trip to Egypt and Israel, so that we could plan the exact itinerary and arrange accommodations for the participants. Time was short, and we knew we had to complete our research before the end of the year.

Although it would be our very first visit to Egypt, neither Ruth nor I were strangers to Israel. Ruth had lived and worked in Israel for about ten years, as a journalist and documentary film producer/director. Her husband was Israeli and their son, Alex, had been born there. Fortunately, she was fluent in Hebrew and had many contacts both in the media and the government. I was not a stranger to Israel either. I had visited the Holy Land at least twelve times prior to meeting Ruth. I considered Israel my spiritual home, although I didn't share that information with Ruth until much later.

Before our journey Ruth approached me and said she wanted to be very up front with me about something that had been troubling her. I encouraged her to tell me what was on her mind.

"You're not going to try to convert me, are you?" she asked earnestly.

"Why would I want to do that?" I answered, surprised by her query.

"Because every born-again Christian I have ever met wanted my soul within ten minutes of finding out I was Jewish," she explained.

"No, I would never do that," I reassured her. "I respect you and your religion and I would never try to convert you."

Ruth breathed a sigh of relief. "I felt I had to ask you that before we launched our project together."

Our departure from Los Angeles in December 1992 proved troublesome. Ruth breezed through the El Al airline security check, but I was obliged to stay behind. They questioned me at length and in depth about the purpose of my mission.

"Why are you going? Where will you stay? For how long?" The agent fired off rounds of questions. "Do you know anybody in Israel? Whom do you know?"

Ruth came to my rescue. She approached the security agent fearlessly.

"Why are you questioning this woman for so long?" she asked. "You can let her go through. She's traveling with me."

"What is your connection to this woman?" he demanded to know.

"We're sisters," Ruth replied. He looked at us, back and forth and forth and back, his gaze sweeping from her white skin to my ebony skin, her blond hair to my dark hair, her green eyes to my brown ones.

"Oh, really," the security agent said, bewildered. "On whose side, your mother's or your father's?"

"On both sides," Ruth retorted.

Only years later, when I became a "daughter" of Abraham and Sarah, would I truly understand the profound significance of her statement.

They waved us on and we boarded the plane.

As a result of a serendipitous meeting with a stranger on the plane, we were directed to a rabbi in Jerusalem who might be able to help us with our plan. The rabbi received us in his office, and we spent three fascinating hours conversing with him.

Sometime in the course of the conversation, Ruth said she thought it was time to give me a Hebrew name. He was quiet for a moment and then suggested the name *Ahuvah*. When I heard it and understood that it meant "beloved," I felt it belonged to me. I practiced saying it out loud. "Ahuvah. Ahuvah." What a beautiful, lilting sound it had!

When we returned to the States at the end of December, Ruth and I had already established the framework for the Festival of Freedom. Now we needed to find participants. It was going to be a difficult task because only three months remained to market the program. Where would the participants come from?

With the support of Pastor Queen of Strait-Way, Ruth and I were able to recruit thirteen participants for the first trip, primarily African-Americans. Dr. Queen and his wife, Phyllis, signed on; Dr. Queen led us in prayer throughout the journey and frequently read Scripture. He had visited Israel many times before and felt at home there.

We arrived in Cairo and on our first morning together gathered to inscribe prayers for peace and freedom on the thirteen-foot silk prayer shawl that Ruth had prepared for us. We went to visit the pyramids of Giza, excited to be there and have an opportunity to retrace the steps of the Exodus as free men and women. One of the participants, Marty, sounded the shofar. Then we wrapped ourselves in the giant prayer shawl and prayed together. (Only later, in my Jewish studies, did I learn that traditionally Jewish men and women pray separately with a *mechitzah* separating them.) We toured Cairo and then took a bus to the interior of the country to visit the Sinai Desert. The energetic members of our group arose before dawn to climb Mount Sinai. The experience of being there, at the site where according to tradition the Ten Commandments were given, created a sensation in me of reconnecting with the world into which the Torah had made its entry, approximately 3,300 years before. I felt that I was walking back through the archives of time.

"There is something very unique about the peace in the Sinai Desert," I observed, as Ruth and I stood together at the foot of Mount Sinai. "There is a special peace in Jerusalem, but I sense a different kind of peace in the Sinai Desert. The two are not the same."

The next day we crossed the Egyptian-Israeli border at Tabah. We passed through Eilat, and continued on what could only be called a breathtaking drive along the Dead Sea. We visited Qumran where the Dead Sea Scrolls were discovered, and we climbed Masada, where legend has it that the Jews in 70 C.E. had chosen to take their own lives rather than become enslaved to the

Romans. Finally we reached Jerusalem, the Holy City. I sang my favorite song out loud. "Jerusalem, O Jerusalem, lift up your voice and sing."

On the first evening of Passover, all participants were invited to celebrate a traditional seder. For the next two days we conducted discussions among peoples of different cultures. There were numerous workshops on the nature of the Passover celebration and the meaning of the ritual foods. On the third evening of Passover and our last evening in Israel, we concluded by celebrating the first "Universal Freedom Seder" which was attended by guests from many lands.

The rabbi led the "seder," wearing a white ceremonial garment (*kittel*). Pastor Queen and his wife sat to his left, Ruth and I to his right. "In the Bible it says thirty-six times that we were slaves in the land of Egypt," he said. "Why thirty-six times? Because there is the danger that we may forget that we were slaves, and if we do we may become insensitive to the suffering of others."

Later at my seminary classes I learned that the Exodus is constantly referred to in everyday prayers, with many deep and fascinating Talmudic explanations.

Upon our return, when he was interviewed by a journalist from the *Los Angeles Times*, Dr. Queen explained his special connection to Judaism. "In order to see the real meaning of Christianity, I must go back to my spiritual roots, trying to get the best information that I can, and I do that by celebrating Passover. The only way to eliminate the friction that is the undercurrent between African-Americans and Jews is through religion...through a deeper knowledge of the God we serve. There is such a commonality between the Jew and the Afro-American; we need to come together because we have suffered frictions in the past. This trip was part of a healing." Ruth and I were very grateful for Dr. Queen's involvement in the tour.

Ruth and I realized that for the second annual Festival of Freedom, we would need to work even more diligently. The greater part of the year had to be spent giving lectures and promoting and organizing the tour. Notwithstanding the enormous commitment required for the pilot project alone, even greater investments of time and effort and money would be required to make the project viable in the future.

Soon after arriving back in America, I resigned from the ministry of Strait-Way and from my position on the board of the women's fellowship. I had spent fourteen years as an ordained minister. I still retained my official license, but it was only gathering dust. I was grateful to Pastor Queen for having introduced me to the Hebrew alphabet and to many aspects of Judaism, but I was ready for more intense study. I enrolled at the Woodland Hills Ulpan, which offered organized Hebrew instruction one evening a week. Because of my incredibly busy schedule and frequent trips away from home, I knew I would be forced to miss some classes. However, I felt that by learning the mother tongue of the Jewish people, I was making an investment in myself and my future. What that future might be was still not clear until one fateful evening.

In May of 1993, upon our return to the States, Ruth invited me to attend a "Shavuot service" with her congregation, B'nai Horin (Children of Freedom). Shavuot is the holiday that comes forty-nine days after Passover, marking the transcendental moment in time when Moses brought down the Ten Commandments and the Torah at Sinai. It was the first time I had ever attended a Shavuot service. Rabbi Stan Levy, the rabbi of B'nai Horin, asked us to close our eyes as he guided us back in time. With his words he recreated the light and sound show that accompanied that divine moment, and I actually experienced the thunder and saw the sky raked by fingers of lightning. When the service ended, I opened my eyes. Ruth and I were standing up, holding hands. I was sobbing.

"I know you won't believe this, Ruth, but I was at Sinai when the Law was given."

My friend looked deeply into my eyes. "Yes, I know," she said. "I know."

At last I understood. My identification with the Law of Moses and the Jewish people was the "missing link." I had finally unlocked the riddle of the peace I had felt in the Sinai Desert.

❋   ❋   ❋

Now that I am a Jew and study Torah, I have a different approach to the way Jews should relate to non-Jews. I now realize our main responsibility to the world is to maintain our special identity and to become a social and spiritual model – a light to the nations. I now celebrate Passover with other Jews, reconnecting to the roots of my people's spiritual heritage. Our task as Jews is to become the people that God has chosen us to be, and in this way we make our universal contribution.

Chapter 5

Broken Dreams

It was January 17, 1994. The day will be forever embedded in my mind. I remember opening my eyes and feeling a bit tired. *I'll just lie in bed a little longer before getting up for prayer*, I thought. I glanced at the clock. 4:32 A.M. I usually prayed at 5:00, because there's something very special about the peace and quiet of dawn. I seem to function more efficiently then, in the calm and serenity of the morning hours.

Suddenly, I was shaken out of bed by the most violent, intense jolting I had ever experienced. At first I thought I was dreaming. Perhaps I was traveling in an airplane and this was bad turbulence. As the ferocity of the shaking continued, I realized it was neither a bad dream nor turbulence. I stumbled out of bed, struggling to retain my equilibrium. The floor was shaking like a roller coaster. Frantically I ran toward the door. Suddenly I fell at the stairwell leading to the loft. The wood-constructed loft was swaying precariously back and forth. When I looked up, it appeared that the entire loft was going to come tumbling down upon my head. I knew this was no dream. This was reality, but it was also the stuff nightmares are made of.

The only thing I could think of as I struggled to gain my footing was Psalm 121. When I finally managed to stand up, I started reciting the psalm: "I lift up my eyes to the mountains: from where will my help come? My help comes from the Lord, Maker of heaven and earth. He will not allow your foot to falter...."

It seemed an eternity until I finally made it to the door. The earth was still shaking so intensely that I couldn't get it open. "Lord, God, my life can't end this way. I haven't fulfilled my purpose in life. I still have a book to write." Again the psalm came to my mind, "The Lord will guard your departure and your arrival, from this time and forever." The door opened.

Although I had reached the "safety" of the outside world, the aftershocks there were just as powerful as the first impact of the earthquake. I ran down the condo stairs and was greeted by the violent screams of a neighbor. Compelled by the intensity of her voice, I ran over and threw my arms around her.

"Are we going to die?" she shouted.

"No," I assured her.

When she finally calmed down, she told me that her husband was out of town on business. "What's your name?"

"Delores."

"I'm Elaine. Thank you for helping me. I was so afraid of being alone."

When I took her hand, she stopped shaking. "Elaine, we're never alone. God is always with us."

We looked for a place of refuge and noticed the other residents huddled together by the steaming Jacuzzi. The morning breeze was chilly, so we didn't wait for an invitation to join them. As we made ourselves at home under the warm blankets kept in storage near the Jacuzzi, I realized that there were some neighbors there whom I had never met. In California, neighbors generally keep to themselves. What a bizarre way to get acquainted! Smiling, I said, "Elaine, I hope that the next time we meet, it will be under better circumstances."

I looked up, and all of a sudden my dear friend Carol Erickson was standing by my side. I was shocked.

Carol's compassion was like life-giving dew to one dying of thirst. The aftershocks were still raging as we embraced.

"Carol, how did you get here?"

"I drove."

"With the ground shaking like this?"

"Yes, it's fun — like being at the carnival."

"I always said you had a great sense of humor, Carol. In my opinion, you deserve an academy award for this performance."

"Look, I was born in California. It's the Wild, Wild West. What's another earthquake?"

By now, our amused onlookers were laughing along with the two of us. I thought for a moment and, risking another sort of aftershock, told Carol the decision I'd just made.

It took the catalyst of an earthquake to shake me out of my comfort zone. I had an international travel business, a newly-constructed condo with top-of-the-line appliances, a leased car, and all manner of material comforts, but something was missing from my life. Of what value were material things to me then? I had spent so many years of my life working to acquire all those things, and then they were taken away in seconds. I felt like King Solomon; all of it was vanity! A definite change had come over me and I was driven to make the major decision of my life. Finally, I would be able to fulfill my dream, to live in Israel and study the Word of God.

"Carol, I'm moving to Israel."

"Oh, you're just a little shaken up. You'll be all right in a few days. Where's your robe?"

I looked at her in amazement, suddenly realizing that she was fully clothed, her shoes perfectly matching her outfit. It hadn't even occurred to me that I was still in my nightgown. Under normal circumstances I would have been embarrassed to leave the cover of the blanket, though everyone else was inappropriately dressed as well. Gratitude sprang up in me as I clung to my long flannel gown, appreciating the little warmth it gave me.

"My robe is upstairs in the rolling hills."

"Do you want me to go upstairs to the rolling hills to get it for you?"

"No, Carol, please go home, and drive carefully."

As she left, tears welled up in my eyes. "What a friend!"

I was terribly worried about my sister. But first, I had to face the music: what had the hollow chords of the last wild movement wrought? When I climbed up to "the rolling hills" and forced open the door of my apartment, I was horrified. Forty-seven years of toil and memories now lay in heaps of dirt and rubble. A feeling of emptiness gripped me as I surveyed the remnants of my life. Every piece of furniture (or what was left of it) had turned over. Dirt from my collection of hanging plants was strewn over my beige carpet; my larger plants, which had been in pots on the floor, were overturned; my decorative pottery shattered. The broken shards broke my composure. *This place is history*, I thought. All my dreams and visions, now crushed, were entangled there among the dirt. Heartbroken, I grabbed a dress, put it over my nightgown, and dug around to find a pair of shoes.

Forget it, I told myself. Just find a right shoe and a left shoe! Now if I could just find my purse with the car keys? Oh, dear God, please help me!

My beautiful bedroom was a wreck. My king-size bed had collapsed onto the floor, with the stuffing of the chamois scattered everywhere. My beloved books were strewn on the floor. My heart sank to my feet. I grabbed one of my Bibles and unearthed my purse from a mound of books.

The bathroom still seemed to be intact. I grabbed my toothbrush, closing my eyes to the shampoo dripping on the counter.

I tried calling my sister, but the lines were down. Quickly, I locked the door and raced down the stairs to the parking garage underneath the condominium complex. "Dear God, I pray to the God of the patriarchs. Please let my sister be okay. I beg you: she's the only one I've got!"

Meanwhile, the aftershocks were still coming. My frantic thoughts kept time with the movement of my feet: *What if my car is smashed? I'll have to walk to my sister's! I have to know that she's okay.*

I was relieved to see that my car was fine. I got in and drove out onto the street. Driving on cracked roads was, as Carol had said, like riding on a roller coaster. None of the traffic lights were working, but since I was the only soul on the street, it didn't really matter. Normally, I would have taken the twenty-minute ride on the freeway. My better judgment led me to take the forty-minute-long surface route.

Anxious to hear the latest news, I turned on the radio. I was horrified to hear that a police officer on a motorcycle had plunged to his death when the freeway had collapsed directly at the junction that I would have taken, where the San Diego and Santa Monica Freeways converged. *Someone is watching out for me,* I assured myself as I struggled to keep control of my car and my nerves.

As I drove over more cracked streets, I thought about Carol

and her example of loving-kindness. Truly only a virtuous woman would be concerned about another's well-being in a life-threatening situation. What a contrast to Elaine, who in her frenzied panic had no way of coping with the earthquake, because she was alone. Reflecting on the past events, I felt sure that God had protected me. Again the words of Psalm 121 came into my mind: "The Lord will guard your departure and your arrival, from this time and forever." Tearfully, I thanked the Almighty.

At last I arrived at my sister's. I could not believe it. Although she lived just a forty-minute drive from the disaster, Nellie came through virtually unscathed. She was fine; her apartment was fine. The only ill she suffered was damage to the hood of her car caused by a falling utility pole.

After we embraced, Nellie asked, "Are you okay?"

Just when I was starting to regain my composure, I had to relive the painful episode again in the retelling.

We tried calling our worried parents, but the telephone lines were still down. Four hours later Nellie finally got through to them.

When I took the phone my mother said, "I know you're all right, but you've got a few bruises." Suddenly, I felt my back and my legs starting to ache. As usual, my mother was right. *How did she know?* Mother continued to speak. "Delores, I suppose you're going to move now."

Brilliance coupled with a prophetic mind! I thought, amazed. "Yes, you know your children very well."

I heard Dad in the background exclaim, "Delores is moving back home!"

"No, Mother, tell Dad I am not moving home.... I am moving to Israel."

There was immediate protest. "You can't move over there — there's shooting and bombing!" But their joy that we had survived another earthquake overshadowed their dismay over my announcement.

Over the ten years I had lived in California I had already been through a number of minor quakes, none as strong as this one. I stayed with Nellie for a few days after the earthquake, until I got the courage and strength to go back and assess the damage. We chuckled over our conversations with our parents. "Isn't it interesting," I observed, "that I am the one who got the bruises, my house was wrecked, and Mother says to you, 'Oh, I wasn't worried about Delores, because she knows the Lord and believes in prayer. I was worried about you.' "

On my drive home I wondered how I'd clean up the debris. I called Henry, my ex-husband, and asked his advice, only to discover that since the earthquake he had been desperately trying to contact me. I told him I was fine, but that I had decided to move to Israel.

We had not allowed the breakup of our marriage to mar the affection we had had for each other since our childhood. Henry had moved from Chicago to California, and started to attend the house of worship where I had previously been on the ministry staff. Although he seemed unsure whether to believe my announcement, he offered to take care of everything: "I'll come by after work to move the furniture back into place. Meanwhile, don't worry!"

True to his word, Henry arrived that evening. Scanning the mess he sighed and said, "Girl, you were right. This place is a disaster."

"Thanks for the compliment," I replied. "I need all the help I can get. I'm leaving for Egypt and Israel in a few weeks." I was taking a Christian tour group to the Middle East in February. The second annual Festival of Freedom was scheduled for just one month later.

The next day, sitting amidst the remaining reminders of the earthquake, I plunged into my usual travel preparations with a renewed sense of urgency.

The twelve days of touring in Egypt and the Holy Land were highly successful. They flew by and once again I was on a return flight home, heading back in a happy frame of mind.

When I opened the door to my home, I couldn't believe my eyes. To my amazement, the condo was immaculate; everything was beautifully arranged. All the repairs needed had been completed. "Thank God," I breathed in relief.

The cracks in the living-room wall had been repaired and painted over. The splits in the wood-beam ceiling at the top of the loft were fixed. Even one of my hanging plants had survived. The beige carpet, which I thought had been destroyed, was now clean and beautiful again. My pink antique sofa and chair were in their usual places. What a blessing! Home sweet home again. My biggest surprise was yet to come: Henry had bought me a gorgeous bouquet of spring flowers. After our marriage had ended, he had kept up the tradition of giving me flowers for my birthday.

I called Henry and thanked him for everything. He made his usual remark, "Are you sure you want to live over there? It's dangerous in Israel, Dee."

"Henry, if you only knew! In which American city can you go walking in the park at night? Israel is really safer than America."

I wondered how my sister was going to feel when I finally moved. I called her to bring her up-to-date, and we arranged to meet each other at the end of the week. I had bought her a beautiful necklace with matching earrings as a gift.

Then I called my parents to tell them I had returned. I was concerned for them and worried how they would react to the day of my final departure for Israel. I thought of Ruth of the Bible. She left her people and her gods, and clung to Naomi. I didn't have a Naomi to cling to. Nevertheless, I did have a family who loved me and respected my decision — even if they didn't completely understand it. They really were displaying loving tolerance!

More ordeals were in store. Shocking news came over the media from Israel that would affect the Festival of Freedom in Jerusalem. Dr. Goldstein, a resident of Kiryat Arba, had just massacred thirty-six Arabs in the Cave of the Patriarchs before being killed himself. This placed Ruth and me in a precarious situation. We wisely decided to cancel the sightseeing tour of Egypt and Israel. Tenaciously determined to continue and succeed, we shifted gears and moved full-speed ahead with a different strategy: We advertised the seder, seminars, and workshops in the *Jerusalem Post*, hoping to interest Israelis.

We arrived in Israel not long before Passover and checked in at a youth hostel, Beit Shmuel, near the Old City. With a few days remaining before Passover, we busied ourselves making appointments with the media. We were fortunate to have the Universal Seder covered by CNN News and receive a cover story with the *Jerusalem Post*.

Exhausted at the end of one of our marathon days, we decided to take a taxi back to Beit Shmuel. Ruth and I had wanted very much to spend the first night of Passover with a family so we would be able to experience a traditional Jewish seder. The taxi driver was a very friendly Moroccan. Ruth began conversing in

Hebrew; I managed to grasp part of their conversation. He said his name was Yossi, and, upon hearing that we needed a place for the seder, he invited us to spend the first night of Passover with his family.

During the flight to Israel, I had been dwelling on a verse in Psalm 119 of my Bible: "There is abundant peace to the lovers of Your Torah, and nothing shall offend them" (vs. 165). This particular verse seemed to be returning to me continually. *The psalm must be coming from out of my soul*, I concluded. I felt at peace both with myself and with God.

Passover finally arrived. Ruth and I slowed down to low gear. We waited outside the hotel; I was clutching a beautiful bouquet of flowers for Yossi's family. Our young host turned up punctually, and we arrived at his home ten minutes later.

When we entered the door, I knew something was wrong. We weren't greeted warmly. Ruth started speaking in Hebrew with the parents and their two daughters.

My Hebrew wasn't that good, but I grasped enough. "Do they want us to leave?" I asked.

Ruth was almost in tears, and the young man was even more distraught than she. "Ahuvah, please give them the flowers." I was still holding the gorgeous bouquet.

Yossi started the ignition outside. I was filled with chagrin. In an amazing feat of self-control, Ruth had managed to maintain her composure in their home. Then she tried to explain.

"Ahuvah, what just happened had nothing to do with you personally. It's because you're a non-Jew. We took the family by surprise. They have no experience with having a non-Jew at a seder, and they were afraid their rabbi wouldn't stay once he arrived."

Yossi was very upset; he could barely speak. "I am so sorry

for this — I don't understand how it could have happened this way."

Suddenly I understood why I was continuously repeating that particular verse of the psalm on the plane. "There is abundant peace to the lovers of Your Torah, and nothing shall offend them." My concern was not for my having been offended; my concern was to console my friends. I exclaimed, "Please don't be upset; nothing can offend me in Jerusalem."

When we got back to the hotel, Ruth went inside to call a family that we had recently met. Earlier, they had invited us for the seder, but Ruth had told them that we were booked. I remained in the taxi with the driver. Ruth was taking so long, I couldn't imagine what was happening. Excusing myself, I went inside to inquire.

It seemed that Ruth had needed more time to compose herself after the experience with Yossi's family. In response to my anxious look she replied, "My dear Ahuvah, I am appalled! How could such a thing happen to you, someone who loves Israel and the Jewish people so much?"

"Ruth, please don't upset yourself. Did this family agree to have us for the seder?"

"Yes."

"Then let's go and celebrate Passover."

Our hosts, Micha and Yael, greeted us warmly when we arrived at their home. Ruth and I were already acquainted with a few of the twenty-five guests, and Yael made the rest of the introductions. Soon we were seated at the table. My heart's desire was for the seder to end so I could go back to our room and make some sense of all the evening's events. Ruth, not realizing that she was opening a Pandora's box, began telling the guests what had transpired that evening.

A guest named Nechama (not her real name) broke into the conversation. "This is our holiday, and I understand that family's response. Pesach is uniquely Jewish, and non-Jews have no right to be at a seder. As a matter of fact, it is halachically very problematic to have a non-Jew at the seder. Pesach is the story of the Nation of Israel's freedom from slavery, our receiving the Torah at Mount Sinai, and becoming a nation. It's our holiday."

Ruth retorted, "There is a universal element in the holiday of Passover which includes freedom for all people."

The debate continued in earnest intensity. In the end, the huge T-shaped table was split down the middle, with about half the people taking one side, and the other half countering them.

The discussion was becoming quite uncomfortable for all present, especially me. There was a momentary silence, and I asked Yael if I could express my feelings. She nodded her consent.

"I would like to say that I am not offended by the family that asked us to leave. If there's a law that prohibits a non-Jew from being at a seder, I had no knowledge of it. I am not angry, and I am not insulted. I am just a bit exhausted. Besides, the Psalmist said: 'There is abundant peace to the lovers of Your Torah, and nothing shall offend them.' Nothing can offend me in Israel."

Tempers were on edge, but at least the parties were being civil toward each other. I didn't even recall where we were in the Haggadah. In all honesty, I really didn't care. I just wanted to go somewhere that was peaceful. Many years later, "Nechama" explained to me what had led her to sparking the debate. This is how she explained what happened:

"[One of the guests] told me that we were going to have a gentile at the seder. Together we pondered the dilemma we would be facing. 'What are we going to do?'

"Another guest remonstrated with us. 'We're going to do absolutely nothing. We're not going to embarrass our host and hostess, or anyone else.' Such was the ambiance of the table that we came to, a feeling of openness, where all concerned knew where they stood.

"But then, when Ruth told us the story — how the family had asked you to leave — there was a covert demand for all those present to say, 'Isn't that terrible, wasn't that racist!'

"To say that the members of the Moroccan family were horrible people is ludicrous. They weren't coming from Mars. They were coming from a Jewish position, as the seder was designed to reinforce Jewish identity and commitment.

"The seder is inherently Jewish, and that's why non-Jews are not invited. Therefore, I tried to speak lovingly to alleviate ignorance, and to express the uniqueness of the Jewish people in a world that sometimes mistakenly perceives our distinctiveness as intolerance or racism.

"The Jewish people have a dual definition: we are a nation that dwells alone, yet our role is to be a light unto the nations. These callings appear to be working in opposite directions; one is isolation, the other is connection. However, they work together. It's only through maintaining our uniqueness that our radiance reaches the world.

"At the conclusion of Ruth's remarks, no one had the courage to argue with her; that's what happens in liberal Judaism. I had to stand up and say, 'This is Judaism.' I couldn't let the silence continue."

When the seder ended, Ruth and I thanked our hosts. The

two of us left, our arms locked together as on previous occasions. We looked at each other and said, "We really are 'Two Women, One Journey!'" We shared a common goal: to bring others closer to God.

"Did you really mean what you said at the table — that you weren't offended?" Ruth asked me.

"Yes, I sure did."

"Well, Ahuvah, my dear friend, I must say that my respect for you has moved up another level."

There is not the slightest doubt that if not for that verse from *Tehillim* — which came to me right when I needed the emotional support — I would not have been able to keep my composure. As rain feeds the earth, seeping into hungry soil and bringing to life everything it touches, a life-giving source of spiritual nourishment was feeding me. As a tender shoot grows from a tiny seed until it finally springs forth from the soil, I too, planted in the fertile ground of my future home, Eretz Yisrael, was constantly growing...and now, slowly but surely, breaking ground!

The next evening, Ruth attended a second seder with family and friends in Tel Aviv. I rested.

Over one hundred people attended the Universal Seder, with our seminars and workshops, on the third day of Passover. Participants were present from more than thirty different countries.

The following day after lunch, Ruth and I went back to the hotel. While we were walking, Ruth threw a bombshell.

"The leader at the second seder said you shouldn't convert."

"What are you talking about, Ruth? I have no intention of converting." I knew I was going through a transition, but certainly nothing that drastic.

Ruth explained, "What he means is that you are a better am-
bassador to the Jewish people the way you are: an African-
American minister who studies Hebrew and loves Israel and the
Jewish people."

"Ruth, I have no idea what you and the rabbi are talking
about." As we continued to walk down the streets of Jerusalem, I
looked at my friend, bewildered. "I have no intention of converting to Judaism. I am a minister, remember?"

"Yes, but you pray three times a day from a siddur, not to
mention your Hebrew name and the rest. Ahuvah, these are Jewish practices."

"Ruth, I can't explain why I do these things; only there is
something very unique about these Jewish prayers. They're so
beautiful. I can't wait until I can pray in Hebrew."

"My dear Ahuvah, you are not the average type, because you
have a special love and fondness for Judaism."

"Don't most people love the Jews?"

"No, Ahuvah my dear, the nations of the world do not love
my people."

It seems that many of the significant events during my journey of faith were connected to Pesach. The rabbi who led the first
seder later introduced me to Rabbi Zev Gotthold, who was instrumental in assisting me with my conversion. I went to the
mikveh only a few weeks before Pesach. And that painful scene
was one of the catalysts for my redemption.

My dear friend Ruth was placed in a difficult situation. On
one hand she was advocating the universal nature of the Passover
seder. On the other hand, we had not been allowed to stay at the
traditional seder because I wasn't Jewish. At that bewildering

time, the two incidents seemed strangely related, and yet so discordant. Oh, how my soul yearned to unlock the riddle of that explosive dialogue.

After much meditating on the affair I realized that the people at the seder who were challenging my right to be there indeed had a point. If gentiles want to discover any universal message in Passover, they have to approach it as a uniquely Jewish holiday. To her credit, Ruth recognized the sensitivities of observant Jews when she explained in our press release that the Universal Seder was scheduled on the third night of Passover, in order to respect the halachic guidelines for the traditional Jewish seder.

On the other hand, there were rabbis in the *chareidi* community who were very upset when they heard that we were asked to leave by the Moroccan family. They felt it was a great desecration of God's Name to invite guests to a home and then to offend them by asking them to leave.

Years later, as an Orthodox Jew, I learned that all this discussion, while interesting theoretically and — at the time — personally painful, was missing the point. A non-Jew is not invited to holiday meals because of a halachic problem with cooking for someone not obligated to be part of the meal. Unlike Shabbos, Jews may cook on holidays, but only to enable them to properly mark the occasion. Thus, on Shabbos, when all cooking must be done in advance, non-Jews may be invited to the meal.

How does one end such a story? The ending is positive: Ruth and I are still very close friends. On her recent visit to Israel, Ruth went to synagogue with me.

During the service, she asked, "You love this, don't you?"

"Yes."

"But there's no interaction between people." I was silent because the chazzan began to daven at that point.

When we left synagogue, Ruth said to me, "You know, that's why many Jews walked away from Judaism; because there's no interaction."

"Ruth, they walked away from a very rich spiritual heritage."

Chapter 6

Moments of Truth

I was thrilled when Shulamit Katznelson, the founder of the Hebrew *ulpan* in Netanyah, personally invited me to enroll in the summer semester. Learning Hebrew would certainly help me fulfill my most cherished dream of living in Israel. We had met Shulamit at her home in Netanyah after the second annual Festival of Freedom. The thought of studying with many diverse people from different countries was exciting. I pondered the thought on the flight back to the States.

When I arrived home in California, I unlocked the door to my condo and kissed my mezuzah, which I had received a few years earlier from Dr. Queen.

A few days later a nice young Jewish man came to my house selling subscriptions to the *Los Angeles Times*. He said he was a high school student earning some extra money in his spare time. I told him I already had a subscription, but thanked him for coming.

Two minutes later the doorbell rang again. It was the same young man.

"Excuse me," he said, "but I noticed that you have a mezuzah. Are you Jewish?"

"No," I replied, "I am Protestant, an ordained minister."

"Can you please tell me why you have a mezuzah?"

"That's a good question." I explained how I attended a house of worship where the pastor taught in Hebrew, observed Passover, and on one of his trips to Israel had bought everyone in the congregation a mezuzah.

"Do you have the Torah verses inside?"

"Yes." I quoted him the verses (Deuteronomy 6:4–9 and 11:13–21).

"I've never heard of such a thing." I could see he was stunned.

"Neither have I. All I can tell you is that there are Christians who genuinely love the Jewish people. I guess I am one of those."

He gave me a big smile and said, "You're a very unusual person. I am happy I met you."

In June, less than two months after Ruth and I had concluded the second annual Festival of Freedom, I returned to Netanyah. It was so exciting to have celebrated my birthday for two consecutive years in Israel. I loved being there, but I was becoming exhausted from the constant traveling back and forth, and I wasn't as young as I had once been. The opportunity to learn Hebrew at a beautiful Mediterranean resort for five weeks, without the usual punctilious attention to tour arrangements, advertising releases, and so on, was just too good to be true. It was an inspirational experience for a minister to be speaking the language of the Bible.

The first week I began practicing saying the prayers in Hebrew, I noticed I was experiencing some sort of spiritual transformation. As I mouthed the holy words, I could feel that the Hebrew letters were affecting me. Something unique was going on within me as I continued learning and speaking the holy language.

After a few weeks, my classmates began discussing the forth-coming fast day. Even though I did not yet understand the sym-bolic meaning of the fast on the ninth day of the Jewish month of Av (called Tishah B'Av), I already realized that there was some-thing intrinsically painful about that day. As I watched the date steadily approaching, I could feel the heaviness weighing down upon me.

Tishah B'Av arrived, and I was experiencing intense pain. In my anguish I called my friend and teacher, Yosef Ben Shlomo Hakohen. Yosef, author of *The Universal Jew*, had started corre-sponding with Ruth after the First Festival of Freedom. We met him the following year, and I found him a wonderful source of in-formation and inspiration. I asked him what the significance of that ominous day was. Yosef, spiritual teacher and *kohein*, an-swered. "Well, Ahuvah, the Jewish people are mourning the de-struction of the First and the Second Temples."

"But how can you explain why I am feeling such anguish? What does this fast have to do with an African-American minis-ter?"

"Are you still praying from your siddur?"

"Yes."

"Then just keep davening, and your answer will come. Be well, Ahuvah. *Shalom.*"

What was I to do with this unexpected piece of advice? All I knew was that for several years I had been praying from a siddur three times a day, going to synagogue on Shabbos, partially ob-serving the laws of Shabbos, and observing the Jewish holidays with Jewish families whenever I had the opportunity. I knew I had to join them on their fast.

I was not a stranger to fasting. I had always felt that my soul was more receptive to spiritual influences during and after the deprivation of food. Some type of spiritual fine-tuning seemed to take place in my life when I fasted; my soul underwent a bit of purification.

Tishah B'Av would prove to be the beginning of many spiritual awakenings. It was difficult for me to fully concentrate on my studies, but I made it through the day. I was relieved when it was over, yet I felt closer to my spiritual roots.

The Shabbos following Tishah B'Av was to have a profound influence on my life. I was praying from my siddur when all of a sudden I became very emotional. I fell down prostrate in the middle of my praying, and exclaimed, "Oh my God, I think I am a Jew!"

It was as if another earthquake had hit the core of my being. A moment of truth had touched my deepest feelings. It explained why I had undergone such emotional and religious turmoil in the past years. My *neshamah*, my soul, was seeking the God of the Jewish people.

When I finally rose to my feet I was a changed person.

How was I going to explain this strange new insight into my spiritual life? Who would believe such a thing? The pieces of the puzzle were falling into place. I began to understand why I had stopped attending services and had started studying my Bible at home on Sundays. I felt a need to discuss this with someone. Perhaps Yosef could help me understand. I made a mental note to call him after Shabbos.

When I called him, Yosef repeated his famous words. "Ahuvah, are you still praying from your siddur three times a day?"

"Yes."

"Ahuvah, just keep on praying."

I hung up the phone, bewildered. I was hoping for a more rational explanation of my situation.

Nine days after Tishah B'Av, I was in class and couldn't stop thinking about Yosef. During a break between classes, I hurried to the telephone and called him. "Yosef, are you okay?"

In a very low, raspy voice, he said he had just learned that his only sister had died. I didn't know what to say or what to do. The only thing I could think of was to quote Psalm 121. When I finished, Yosef thanked me and said, "Ahuvah, that's one of my favorite chapters of *Tehillim*."

"Is there anything more I can do?"

"No, just keep my family in mind when you're praying."

The following day I took a minibus from Netanyah to Jerusalem. Yosef had told me how fond he was of his neighborhood, so I looked forward to seeing Bayit Vegan for the first time.

When I arrived at Yosef's building, I couldn't find the entrance to his apartment. "Yosef, Yosef, it's Ahuvah," I called. "Where are you?"

"I am down here, Ahuvah. Go back out and down the stairs." I could hear his voice through a small window.

When I walked down the stairs the door was open, and I saw him in the company of other visitors. I couldn't believe my eyes. Yosef was sitting on a very low chair, almost on the floor. His shirt was torn, and his hair wasn't combed. It was like taking a walk back through the archives of time. I had read in the Bible about what people did during their mourning, but never imagined that with my own eyes I would see anyone still following those customs.

Yosef, even during his bereavement, started to teach me. My heart warmed, knowing I was with that true Jewish soul who had always been so kind and helpful to Ruth and me.

"Ahuvah, when one is making a shivah call, it's customary not to greet the mourner, but to wait and let the mourner himself initiate the conversation. He will usually share with the visitor something about his departed loved one."

He then began to tell me about his beloved sister, Devorah (Dorothy) Oboler, who'd passed away from various complications related to the muscular dystrophy that she had suffered from throughout her adult life. Although she had a painful disability that caused her to be homebound, he told me, she had a joyful spirit that was a source of life and light for others. When she was in a hospital for the disabled, she would go in her wheelchair to visit those patients who couldn't leave their beds. She was able to see the hearts and souls underneath the broken bodies, and through her love and respect, they rediscovered their own worth and dignity.

Devorah helped organize a Shabbos morning gathering for the Jewish patients. Her compassion was also expressed through her poetry. She often wrote about the suffering and loneliness of the homebound elderly and disabled, and she sent her poems to friends and former classmates. Her poetry also inspired them to begin visiting the homebound in their own neighborhoods.

In Far Rockaway, a group of Orthodox women visited Devorah and other disabled people and provided them with meals. They thought very highly of Devorah's poetry and published her work in their newsletter. A year before she passed away, Devorah received a special honor from the members of her Bais Yaakov graduating class. They asked her to be the guest speaker at the class reunion, and they hired a limousine to bring her to the gathering in the Boro Park neighborhood of Brooklyn. They also distributed beautifully printed copies of Devorah's poems. She spoke to them about the dignity and value of the elderly and disabled who are often forgotten by the community, and she urged them to become pioneers in the mitzvah of caring and honoring those precious human beings.

"She herself was a precious human being and is missed by all who knew her."

I thanked Yosef for sharing such warm memories of his sister with me.

When I left Yosef that day I was amazed. Even in the height of his mourning for one of his closest relatives and his only sibling, he was still performing his role as a *kohein* and spiritual teacher. I was in awe of his inner strength and how he coped with death and separation. His attitude toward death was not something based merely on emotionalism, but on the honor bestowed on the eternal souls of the loved one.

"Dear God," I confided in my Maker, "I don't know why You have chosen to show me all these things, but there really is something unique about the Jewish people."

I couldn't wait to telephone Ruth. I found the nearest pay phone and related the entire experience to her.

"Please give him my condolences when you speak to him again," Ruth said. "I'll mail him a card in the meantime. How is his neighborhood? Is it as lovely as he described it?"

"Yes, Ruth, it's as beautiful as he said. And you know, all the men here wear black suits. It's *chareidi* — it's a 'black' neighborhood."

Always on my wavelength, she said, "Then you should feel at home!"

Happy to close the afternoon on a light note, I said, "As a matter of fact, I do."

We both laughed, and I went to catch the bus back to Netanyah.

Before his sister died, Yosef had introduced me to a very special American couple who lived in the Jerusalem neighborhood of Old Katamon, Rabbi Mordechai and Avigail Goldberg. They invited me to stay with them for Shabbos.

After enjoying their happy family atmosphere, I grew anxious about my own family. I had spoken with my parents only a week before, but it seemed much longer. At the first opportunity, I called my sister to see how they were.

"Lobo" (that was Nellie's special name for me), "I am very worried about Mother. I called yesterday, and she had fallen down three times."

Oh, no, I thought. *I can't handle another crisis, not now.*

While my sister was conference-calling my parents, I took emotional stock of myself. My resources for dealing with new shocks to the system had plummeted to level zero. Every night since Tishah B'Av I had gone to bed sobbing, unable to figure out what was going on in my life. During the day, when I'd be sitting in *ulpan* learning Hebrew, my emotional heartthrobs were like fiery darts going through my body. There were some days when my knees were so weak that I felt I needed crutches. In my own world of uncertainty, I could hear my mother's voice reverberating, "Delores, God is going to do something very special in your life."

Suddenly her voice became a reality. "Oh, it was nothing. I kind of lost my balance. How are your studies progressing?" Just the way I expected it to be! My mother was more concerned with my Hebrew studies than her own welfare.

"Would you like me to come home?"

"No. Don't you stop your studying! Stay there and learn. I know you love what you're doing, and you sound so happy every time we speak."

On the conference-line with my mother and sister, I asked God to strengthen our mother. Whenever Mother and I talked on the phone, I always closed with a word of prayer. "Amen, Delores. I feel so much better. Your prayers are so inspiring."

"It's all from God, Mother."

As Mother went to get Dad, I told Nellie to stay on the line.

"I don't like the way she sounds," Nellie said. "Lobo, I think we should fast."

"Nellie, could you try fasting without water if you can? It's more powerful that way."

"I've never gone without liquids. I don't know if I can do that."

"Okay, Nellie, just do your best and God will do the rest. Call me when it's over." As usual, we synchronized our watches and designated the time.

I do not advise fasting while trying to learn Hebrew. I could barely concentrate in class the next day, but I viewed it as just another challenge. I quoted every psalm and every Biblical verse I could think of. Then I laughed inwardly, remembering all those great sermons I used to preach, such as "Man's Extremity Is God's Opportunity" and "He Gives Me Strength in the Midst of the Storm." Now I was faced with an opportunity to apply one of those sermons to my personal circumstances. Then I could do a follow-up sermon on "How I Got Over...."

Netanyah is a very lovely sea resort, resting on the Mediterranean, but it's extremely humid in the summer. As I sat in class the next day fasting, I comforted myself by saying, "This, too, will pass."

I was happy when we broke for lunch. As I passed a few of my friends, they called, "Ahuvah, aren't you coming to join us?"

"No," I said. "I'm going to lie down until the afternoon classes."

Once in my room, I was relieved to have some peace and quiet. Rather than take a nap, I decided to just sit and pray quietly for my mother. While meditating on Mother's situation, I took strength recalling the time that Grandmother had recovered from her aneurysm after the entire family had fasted for her.

I called this strict discipline a "divine assignment." A dear friend from my ministry days, Shirley Jensen (not her actual name), once fasted with me for seven days.

The first day I fasted without water. After that, I asked my friend, "Are we going to make it through this thing alive?"

Shirley laughed, "Yes, Delores, we'll make it. I've done it numerous times. But you have to pray."

Shirley introduced me to a pure way of finding spirituality. She never really asked anyone how to pray or which was the best way. With a childlike faith, she believed that if we asked God for anything according to His will, He would do it. Believe it or not, I actually did survive the seven-day fast.

The day of my mother's fast finally ended. I went straight to my room, took a shower, said a brief prayer to God asking Him to heal my mother, and prepared for bed.

The morning after a fast, I usually wasn't hungry, so I had a very light breakfast.

Then I went to call my sister. Her words were music to my

ears: "Boy, are those prayers working over there! Did you go to the Western Wall?"

"No," I replied. "The land is holy, Nellie, and the God of the Patriarchs is faithful."

"Wait," she said, "I'll get Mother on the telephone. You won't believe this!"

When she put me on hold, I said to myself, "Yes, I will believe it. God is so wonderful."

"Hello, Delores." My mother's voice was full of life and joy.

"Mother, thank God, you sound great!"

"I feel fine. I think it was just the hot weather."

"I am so happy that you are better. It's not so easy for me to be so far away from home when you're not feeling well. But guess what! Ruth and I have a lecture tour in October. We'll be in Green Bay, Wisconsin, Milwaukee, and Chicago. So I'll get to see you and Dad!"

"Well, you hurry home. We miss you."

At the conclusion of the semester at Ulpan Akiva, in mid-August, I was looking forward to being in Israel for the New Year and Sukkos holidays for the very first time. The Moriah Hotel, as a member of the hotel chain where all my groups stayed, gave me a special rate for six weeks, and upgraded me to a suite.

Once back in Jerusalem with my friends, I was able to relax and unwind. It was so wonderful to have a view of the Old City — I thought I had died and gone to heaven!

I was perplexed about how to prepare myself for the Jewish holidays. Could the Goldbergs perhaps be of some assistance? I wondered.

The neighborhood of Old Katamon was just a twenty-minute walk from the Moriah Hotel. I called the Goldbergs and

Avigail answered. "*Shalom*, Ahuvah. It's good to hear from you. How's your Hebrew coming along?"

"*Ani midaberet Ivrit ketzat* (I speak Hebrew a little)," I responded.

We both laughed. "That's a good start, Ahuvah. When are you coming to us for Shabbos?"

"Thank you so much for asking. That's an answer to my prayer. Soon, I hope. Avigail, is there anything I need to do to prepare myself for the holidays of Rosh HaShanah and Yom Kippur?"

"No, not really. Are you going to fast on Yom Kippur? The Jewish people fast on Yom Kippur, but you're not obligated, because you're not Jewish."

I told Avigail that I was determined to fast. Besides I had heard so much about this holiday I wanted the optimum of what could be gained. Fasting wasn't difficult for me, and besides, I would be staying in my hotel room most of the day.

"In any case, you can eat with us on the two days of Rosh HaShanah," Avigail offered. "The children will be happy to see you again. Oh, Ahuvah, you may want to purchase a Metsudah *Selichos*, since you love the prayers so much. It's a special book with repentance prayers that we recite before the High Holy Days."

The next day I bought my own *Selichos*. Rabbi Mordechai spent time with me the following Saturday night explaining the *Selichos* and how they represented *teshuvah*, repentance.

"*Teshuvah* means to repent. We review what we have done during the last year, and we try to evaluate and better our relationship with God and with people. Rosh HaShanah is the day that we, the Jewish people, crown God King."

I don't recall whether I fully understood everything that Mordechai said, but it certainly sounded good. Avigail told me when I should start praying from my *Selichos* prayer book. I felt my life was being transformed when I completed the special prayers for the lead-up to the Jewish New Year and the Ten Days of Awe (the period encompassing Rosh HaShanah and Yom Kippur).

I remember my feelings that first day of *Selichos*. Reading those prayers was like undergoing spiritual surgery without anesthesia. That's the only way I can describe it. I asked myself, *Is this what teshuvah is?*

The eve of Rosh HaShanah arrived. As I walked from the hotel to the Goldbergs, my heart was full of gratitude. I was grateful to the Almighty for bringing me to Jerusalem. I was thankful for all the wonderful families I had met, and especially thankful for how loving and accepting everyone was. There seemed to be something so mystical about walking down the streets of Jerusalem. I reflected in my heart on the numerous sermons of repentance I had preached to others. This time, in the Holy City of God, I had encountered *teshuvah* personally.

I entered an Orthodox synagogue for the first time in my life. It was different from any other place I had ever worshiped at, and my first impression was that it was authentic and unique. The women sat separated from the men, and I noticed that most of the women had their hair covered. Concerned that I didn't have a Kleenex or handkerchief, let alone a hat, I asked Avigail if I needed to cover my head.

"No, no," she answered with a smile. "Only married women are obligated to cover their hair." I also noticed that everyone had a special prayer book called a *machzor*, so I knew I had to buy one for the following year. The most impressive thing there was that everyone was extremely quiet and serious. I felt I should be the same. To tell the truth, I really didn't know what I was doing, but I felt secure, assured that I was in good hands. Mordechai was the cantor, and because I was familiar with his voice I was able to follow the service fairly well.

"*Shanah tovah, chag sameiach*," Mordechai and Avigail told people as we left the synagogue. I noticed that even the children were saying it, so I greeted everyone in the same manner.

"Did you enjoy the evening, Ahuvah?" Mordechai asked me.

"I don't have adequate words to describe how I feel," I answered candidly. "I need time to digest all of this."

When we came home I asked, "Mordechai, what does '*shanah tovah*' mean?"

" 'A good year,' " he replied. "And '*chag sameiach*' means 'happy holiday.' "

Our festive meal was lovely. As I looked at the charming table, the first thing to catch my eye was a fish head. Before I could ask the obvious question, Mordechai explained that the food of that evening was symbolic for the Jewish people for the coming year.

The men would partake of the head of the fish to indicate that they should be the head, and not the tail. I breathed a sigh of relief when Mordechai said that I didn't need to eat it. Fish heads had always seemed so repulsive to me.

For some reason I had an eerie feeling that the eyes of the fish were staring at me the entire evening. The children, Hanni, Yitzchak, Efraim, and Ruchama, chuckled heartily when I told them my thoughts. Whatever discomfort I had with fish heads, it did not deter me from enjoying all the new foods prepared especially for the evening. Mordechai explained the meaning of these *simanim*, symbols, in order. Before I left, he invited me to join them at their friends' home for their *yom tov* meal the next day. It was extremely thoughtful of them to include me, a stranger, in all their family plans.

Walking back to the hotel, I said to myself, "This is fascinating. I have never had such a spiritual elevation of my soul in my entire life. It is Divine Providence that I am here in Jerusalem for my first High Holy Days."

Up to that point, I had been very impressed with the lives of the Jewish people. That night, I felt I had finally arrived. Even though I didn't understand what any of it meant, I had still learned something special. The Jewish people were reciting my mother's favorite psalm, Psalm 27, twice a day from the beginning of the penitential month of Elul until the end of the Sukkos holiday. The rest of the services were still confusing, but given time, I was sure I would come to understand Judaism better.

"*Shanah tovah, chag sameiach*," I greeted the hotel clerk as I entered the door.

At synagogue the next morning, I noticed that the men were wearing talleisim. When they got to the part in the service where the Holy Ark was opened, my heart leaped with joy. I thought I was going to pass out! I knew the Torah rested there; I knew that God's Word was holy, that the Ark was holy, and that I was in the Holy City of God.

When they started singing *Avinu Malkeinu*, "Our Father, Our King," I thought the heavens were going to open up. It was the most beautiful song I had ever heard in my life!

After the reading of the Torah there was the blowing of the shofar. It was the first time I had ever heard a shofar blown in a synagogue. I was fascinated, though I had no idea what it meant. In my mind, I could envision the appearance of a king. It was such a spectacular event, in a spiritual sense — who could believe it? What a privilege to have been given the opportunity to be present!

While the Torah was being carried to the Ark, I immediately recognized the psalm the congregation was singing. It was my father's favorite, Psalm 24. *How incredible*, I thought, *to hear my mother's favorite psalm at the conclusion of the evening service, and now Psalm 24, my daddy's.* I felt a tugging at my heart.

Yom Kippur was approaching; it was to be the first time I would fast on that holiest of days. While eating my last meal for the next twenty-five hours, I wondered what it would be like. The walk to the synagogue seemed so strange. The streets were absolutely silent, with an other-worldly serenity and calm.

The synagogue was enveloped in the same remarkable peace and quiet I had felt walking through the streets. The cantor began to chant a soft melody called *Kol Nidrei*. Every Hebrew word seemed to penetrate my soul and cleanse it of all residue. I was completely divested of anything from my past. Spiritually, I knew what was going on, but to verbalize it would take years and much more spiritual fine-tuning.

I sobbed uncontrollably throughout the entire length of the singing. When I finally stopped, I looked around for Avigail. There wasn't a face that I recognized. A lovely lady standing next to me motioned wordlessly, as if to ask, "Is there anything I can do?"

"No, I can't explain this. There's nothing you can do," I answered aloud. I didn't know at that time that one shouldn't talk during *Kol Nidrei*. *Baruch Hashem*, now I know.

To console me, my newfound friend put her arm around my

shoulder and gave me a warm embrace. That was exactly what I needed. I looked at her, and we exchanged smiles. There was no need for words. I couldn't explain to her or anyone else what was happening inside of me. Although it was the first time in my life I had heard the melody, it was as though my *neshamah* knew *Kol Nidrei*. I had no idea at the time that the prayer was a declaration of the nullification of past and future vows and oaths, but at that moment I felt my soul experiencing something that I had been awaiting my entire life. Much later, I figured out what was going on: by nullifying all my previous commitments, I was enabling my soul to return to its Jewish roots.

When I left the service that night, I wished the other congregants a "*chatimah tovah*," blessing them that they would be inscribed and sealed in the Book of Life for the next year. I felt I was saying it as a Jew. I walked down the street knowing that I would never forget that night as long as I lived. The peace that lingered in the air on my way back to the hotel surpassed all my understanding. I couldn't hear a bird; there were no planes, no cars. Even the leaves on the trees weren't moving. I said to myself very softly, "I know who my God is. This is what it will be like when Mashiach comes. The peace of the Almighty is in this place."

The essence of my new realization gripped me. In my bliss, I began reciting the prophet Isaiah, chapter 40, which I knew and loved: "Every valley will be raised, and every mountain and hill will be lowered; the crooked will become straight and heights will become valley. The glory of God will be revealed, and all flesh together will see that the mouth of God has spoken." I felt those holy words depicted what had happened in my life. Every valley – the doubts and worries – had been raised. The mountains – the haughtiness, the feeling of pride – had been lowered.

Crooked places represented the places I had traversed where I hadn't belonged. The heights of conceit had been leveled to valleys. Only God's glory was imminent in my life. Only Hashem's glory!

As I continued to bask in the serenity and peace, it suddenly occurred to me that I had been headed down this path my entire life. It had taken me forty-eight years to search and seek out the truth. I thought of all the endless researching and running to find cross-references in order to understand Bible verses. The years of sleepless nights spent pondering the Bible and things that seemed unfathomable had culminated in a beautiful crescendo with the sound of *Kol Nidrei*, the haunting chant that struck the chords of my heart. I knew that my God was real! It all made sense — the little game I used to play when I first started studying the Bible. My childish game of Abraham being my great-grandfather, and my walking hand-in-hand with him the breadth and length of the Holy Land, had come true. The event I had hoped for my entire life had arrived.

The words of Ruth to Naomi which I had read so many times before in my Bible were now my words: "For wherever you go, I will go; where you lodge, I will lodge; your people are my people, and your God is my God." The Jewish people were my people.

I thought about my personal connection with the service in the synagogue, and how my parents' favorite psalms were such a significant part of the prayer. How many Jews from birth would be able to tell such a story? My father led me to the Torah with Psalm 24, and my mother carried me with Psalm 27. Who would believe that the granddaughter of sharecroppers from Mound Bayou, Mississippi, would become a Jewess? And all with the help of the book of Psalms.

How was I going to explain this to my family? I knew my mother would understand. She had always encouraged me in everything that I attempted to do in life. My mother was my best friend. Surely, she would understand! Then it hit me. What if she didn't understand? What if...? I decided to abandon the thought. Why worry about the future? I cherished every second as I quoted *Tehillim* and focused on the quietness and the peace of the Holy Day I was privileged to enjoy. Where else in the world could you experience such an awesome phenomenon, except in Jerusalem?

I spent most of the remainder of Yom Kippur quietly studying my Bible in the hotel room. I walked back to synagogue for the closing service, *Neilah*. The blowing of the shofar marked the conclusion of one of the most unforgettable days of my life.

The next morning I called Rabbi Mordechai and Avigail to tell them that I was converting to Judaism. They didn't seem too surprised. They immediately wished me *mazal tov*, but Rabbi Mordechai asked, "Are you sure you want to do that, Ahuvah? Have you really left behind your previous spiritual path?"

I carefully considered his probing question — what a heavy one it was! At that moment, I didn't know how many countless times and in how many countless different ways I would be hearing that same question. For as long as I could remember, the decisions of my life were made only after praying and studying the Word of God. Repeatedly when I stood at the crossroads of life, the particular Scripture verse that was the answer to my need would penetrate my soul. To me, there was never any question about there being a clear answer in every situation. I just knew that it was my responsibility to pray and search God's Word to find the right path.

With my making the momentous decision to join the Jewish people, I knew my path would be changed. I knew Hashem's wisdom was contained in His Torah. That Torah He had given to the Jewish people, who were committed to fulfilling the laws and commandments, valuing them even above their very lives. My feelings at the time were clear: As a candidate for conversion and a Jewess, I would become more strongly enlightened and committed to the truths of this world.

My next step was to call Yosef to inform him. I didn't understand why he didn't seem surprised either. What seemed obvious to my friends had taken me a long time to realize.

The next morning I was awakened by a lot of noise. It sounded like hammers were banging all over the place. I looked out the window and saw little huts being constructed. *It's a sukkah!* I marveled. *They're gorgeous.*

During Sukkos I was delighted to see the beautifully decorated sukkos in every yard. When I sat and dined in the Goldbergs' sukkah, I was reminded of our family outings in my childhood, with barbecues in the park.

The culmination of the holidays was Simchas Torah. It was, in some way, the most exhilarating day of the holiday period. The singing and dancing around the Torah reminded me of a favorite Bible story of King David dancing around the Ark of the Covenant after it had been retaken from the Philistines.

After the Jewish holidays, it was extremely difficult to return to the seemingly mundane things of the physical world. Spiritually, I was still on the mountain. I had heard everyone talk about how exciting it was to be in Jerusalem for the Jewish holidays. Now I could fully share their sentiments! When it was time for me to leave, as much as I missed my family, I had no desire to.

Jerusalem was my home, and I felt the peace of the Almighty everywhere my shoes trod.

I was compelled to shift my attention to my friend Ruth and the Festival of Freedom. We had lectures and speaking engagements in the States with one place of worship and many synagogues, and I was no longer a practicing ordained minister. I would have to discuss with Ruth how we would deal with my new set of circumstances.

I found Los Angeles to be like a foreign country. Although I had just arrived, I couldn't wait to start the enormous task of sorting out all my personal belongings for my departure, which was set for March, 1995. By the time Ruth and I would conclude the third Festival of Freedom, I would hopefully be living in my new home in Jerusalem.

I scurried to check my messages and return phone calls.

"You're home!" my sister cried ecstatically when I called her.

"Yes, but not for very long. Ruth and I have the lectures coming up, and then I have to start packing to move." I decided not to tell my sister that I was converting because I knew she would react strongly and emotionally. I hoped that after I informed my parents, they could advise me on how I should break the news to the rest of the family.

I wasn't sure how to dissolve my partnership with Ruth and how much to tell of my conversion plans. My worries were for nothing, though. When we met, it was as if she already knew my latest decisions. I brought her up-to-date on the entirety of my four-month visit to Israel and explained that I still wanted to honor and keep my word and fulfill my responsibilities. We made a short-term decision to continue with the third annual Festival of Freedom. We just had one commitment left with a house of worship, and that we canceled because of my new religious convictions. The rest of our speaking tour, to Green Bay, Wisconsin, Milwaukee, and Chicago, proceeded on schedule.

We stayed with Ruth's sister, Leah, in Green Bay and lectured to the Jewish congregation where Leah worshiped. Whenever we spoke, Ruth and I showed the CNN video about the Festival of Freedom. Then we would speak briefly about our joint venture, leaving time for questions and answers. Frequently, we were encouraged by our audiences' enthusiastic responses to the universal theme of the Festival of Freedom. The clock was winding down and I knew that the end of our project was approaching. It was a good feeling to know that we had done such a great job.

From Green Bay we flew to Milwaukee, and from there on to Chicago.

"Chicago, Chicago, that toddling town." The lyrics were familiar to both of us. It was very exciting to be visiting my parents. But sadness gripped me with the knowledge that my brother Rennie would no longer be meeting me at the airport.

I remember Rennie's death vividly. It happened in the spring of 1991. The doctor had a long medical term for an enlarged heart that had stopped beating. His words meant nothing to us. What we knew was that my beloved baby brother, Rennie, was dead at the age of thirty-three. We were devastated by the tragedy. Though we kept our faith, my mother never seemed quite the same afterwards.

At the funeral, my mother's familiar words echoed in my heart: "I hope I die before my children." After his passing she would repeatedly say, "You have no children, Delores. You have no idea what this is like." The only way I knew to comfort her was with my prayers.

Lorenzo "Rennie" Buckner was the joy of our lives. Whenever I saw him, he always had a smile on his face. I remember how he loved baseball and football. In college, he'd actually been drafted by the Chicago Bears, his lifelong dream. How shattered he'd been when he was cut! But all of us loved him. We didn't care whether he played football or not.

Rennie was a husky kid, but extremely sensitive and gentle. Whenever I flew into Chicago, I knew I could always depend on him to be at the airport on time to pick me up. He loved music and was an accomplished guitarist and drummer. There were times when I would call him long-distance, and he would say, "I just composed a song. Would you like to hear it?" But the most wonderful thing about my little brother was that he was always smiling.

When Rennie died, our family was devastated. His wife, Eileen, who loved him dearly, survived him with three beautiful children, Shaina, Isaiah, and Leonard. I had planned to devote a whole chapter of this book to Rennie, but it was so painful that I had to relinquish the idea. The memory of his love and warmth for his wife and children and the rest of his family will forever be embedded in my heart.

My memories, both sad and bittersweet, were interrupted by the flight attendant announcing the landing. Ruth woke up just in time. We rented a car at the airport and went straight to our hotel.

My parents were overjoyed with our arrival and booked us for dinner for the second night. I hadn't seen my parents since the last Mother's Day, and waited in anxious anticipation. As we drove through my old neighborhood, I saw that it had continued to deteriorate into the squalor of yet another black ghetto. Oh, how I wished they would move. They could afford to live in a much better neighborhood. But I guess they preferred to remain where they were comfortable and knew the neighbors.

Mother had fixed a great meal for us. After dinner, we sat leisurely in the den, and I hesitantly broached the topic that was uppermost in my mind. "Well, Mom and Dad, you know I am planning to move to Israel in March," I began. They nodded, little knowing where this was leading. "In addition to moving," I continued, "I am planning to convert to Judaism."

There was complete silence.

I started explaining to them what that entailed. "I will have to attend a seminary and study. But I'll be studying the Bible in Hebrew, and you know how much I love to study the Bible."

Mother gazed at me with a look that pierced my insides. "Delores, I know that any decisions you made about God you thoroughly investigated."

Dad added, "I hope that you have seen things in my life that helped influence your decision."

Encouraged by this response, I started telling them about the exciting things that had happened during my four-month visit.

When I finished my mother said, "We're very proud of you. I noticed that every time you go to Israel, you seem to be so different, so happy. But Delores, you be careful over there!"

We hugged each other tearfully, Mother, Dad, and me. Ruth was at her favorite position — behind the camera lens. She had filmed the entire moving episode!

Soon Ruth and I were on the freeway back to the hotel. When we left Chicago, I had no way of knowing that this would be the last time I would be seeing my mother alive. She was sixty-nine at the time and gorgeous, still without wrinkles.

When I returned to California, I was relieved to have the emotional and sensitive issues taken care of. I had just five months to pack up forty-eight years of my life. It had taken me nine months to regroup from the dynamics of the earthquake. All surplus items that weren't needed for Israel were to be given away. I knew I wouldn't have a spacious flat; psychologically I now made the adjustment. I didn't know how I was going to support myself in Israel or where I was going to live. But that didn't deter me. It was going to take a miracle to sort out all those things. *Well,* I thought, *they always said I was a woman of great faith. Here I go again.*

Calling shipping companies and buying large boxes was first on the agenda. I divided my many books into piles — some to ship and some to give away. I did the same with my clothes and shoes. When I got to the kitchen area, things were simpler. Thanks to the earthquake, the majority of my china and crystal were gone. Only a few crockery items were left to start a household.

With all the major things taken care of, I indulged myself by reading *To Be a Jew* by Rabbi Haim HaLevy Donin. I cried throughout the entire book. The chapters about Shabbos and the Jewish holidays reminded me of all the wonderful experiences I'd had. Four incredible months in Israel, with people who actually lived their daily lives according to the guidelines of *To Be a Jew,* had made a deep impression on me. The chapter about "sitting shivah" reminded me of Yosef.

One Sunday morning, nearly two months after my return from Chicago, I picked up the telephone and dialed home. According to my watch, Mother should have been at Sunday services, but a strange intuition told me that she would be home.

"Hello, Mother, why aren't you at service?"

"Oh, I just felt like resting today."

I asked her how Rennie's children were.

"We were just over there," she said, "and I cooked chicken with rice and gravy and baked a pound cake."

Mom and I chatted a little while longer. Then I said, "Okay, Mom, let's have prayer."

I finished my prayer and said, "God bless you, Mother. I love you."

"I love you, too. Goodbye."

I was used to closing my phone conversations with Mother with a prayer. However, this prayer was different. I hung up the telephone and asked myself, "Where is she lately? She hasn't been the same since Rennie died."

Early the next morning, just after I had finished praying, I received a phone call from my brother Ezra.

"Hello, Lobo." His voice sounded like it was coming through a long tunnel. "How are you doing?"

"I just finished praying."

There was a long pause. I waited for him to get to the point.

"Mother just died."

"Are you joking?"

"No, Delores, would I joke about a thing like this?"

"Where was she?"

"At home. She died in her sleep."

"Where's Dad?"

"He's at home." Then came the inevitable. "You'll have to tell Nellie."

"Don't worry, she's been calling me every day." My sister was away in Tokyo, on tour, working as wardrobe manager for the entertainer Donna Summer.

After hanging up I started praying again. I walked through my home quoting my mother's favorite psalms.

The telephone rang again. It was my sister.

"Hello, Delores. I called home and asked Dad if I could speak to Mother. He said to call you. What's going on?"

"Nellie, I don't know how to tell you this, but Mother is dead."

Even though Mom was gone, I knew that her second husband would always be Dad to me. I took stock of myself before I phoned him.

"Hello, Dad, how are you?"

He was crying.

"I know this is a very hard time for you," I said.

"Yes, we were happily married for so many years."

"Yes, I know. Have you started to make any of the burial arrangements?"

"Not yet."

In a few days I was airborne again. Ruth had offered to come with me, but I didn't see the point in her leaving her family again. As I flew into Chicago alone, I couldn't enjoy the beautiful skyline that I loved so much. I was in too much pain.

My mother, Christine Franklin Gray, was buried on December 23, 1994. Encouraged by my sister, I called upon my remaining emotional strength to eulogize our mother. A patent measure of her strength was that my mother encouraged each of her children to pursue the desires of their heart — her mature and noble, selfless reaction to my decision to convert was the most shining example of that. I emphasized the courage and strength of my mother, her acts of loving-kindness throughout our years of growing up. I told the other mourners how our home was a haven to all manner of wayfarers.

To this day I have no idea how I eulogized my mother; I think I was just on automatic pilot. The funeral over, I went back to Los Angeles and continued my packing. The next morning, I knew I had to prioritize my time. With a bare three months left, the countdown for my departure to Israel was in full swing. My mother would certainly not have wanted me to focus on my distressed emotional state at that time. I collected whatever fortitude and spiritual stamina I could muster and concentrated on what was needed to build myself a new spiritual and geographical home.

Ruth was a wonderful comfort to me during the following months. She had performed a role-reversal, from friend to mother. There were occasions when it was much needed. We still had newspaper interviews, lecture tours, seminars, and workshops, during which time I was in the worst pain I had ever experienced in my life. I didn't even know how I was standing on my feet.

My schedule hadn't allowed me time to mourn properly. Since Mother's death, I hadn't experienced any real peace; I just worked automatically, without any real feelings. If only the pain would go away! As much as I loved to pray, it appeared that even prayer wasn't helping to ease the pain in my heart.

My mother's birthday was coming up in March. Her birthday gift, a photo album which I had specially designed for her in pink satin and lace, was still in my luggage. When the day of my departure for Israel arrived, Mother had been gone for three months. The worst part was that I hadn't even cried; the tears just didn't come. How I wished I could cry.

❋   ❋   ❋

If I have been blessed with a mother of unusual spiritual strength of character, I have been fortunate, also, to have found a "spiritual mother" of great stature, Rebbetzin Chaya Heyman from my Jerusalem neighborhood of Bayit Vegan. When I first told Rebbetzin Heyman of my intention to convert to the Jewish faith, she exclaimed, "Are you crazy?" I was aware that it is traditional for Jews to discourage converts at the beginning stage in order to test their sincerity. "Why on earth would you want to burden yourself with the six hundred and thirteen mitzvos when you don't need to?" she continued. "You can still merit great reward by observing the seven commandments of Noah."

I told her that despite so much advice to the contrary I had to pursue my heart's desire to be a Jew. She seemed to understand that I was determined.

But the following morning when I sat down next to her in shul, a Christian with an ArtScroll siddur, the full impact of the situation hit her. She became a nervous wreck when we began the morning prayers. I looked at her expectantly, waiting for her to show me where to start. Marshaling her resources, she began the task. It was quite difficult because she couldn't talk in the middle of prayer, only turn my pages and use sign language. Somehow we managed to get through and enjoy the service.

After a few weeks of my initial siddur training, she began teaching me the guidelines of the *Shemoneh Esrei*. When she noticed that I was stepping backward on the wrong foot, she poked me and motioned the correct way with hers. After several weeks of daily confusion I was so embarrassed that I cried, "Hashem, please help me remember the right foot."

Chapter 7

I Did It My Way

I wondered if there would ever be an end to those loaded missiles my family and friends constantly hurled at me. "How will you get around in Israel? You don't have a car anymore. How can you give away all your furniture and brand-name appliances and everything else you worked so hard for? Do you have enough money to sustain yourself? Delores, how will you earn a living? You lost thousands on your condo. Don't you feel you've taken a tremendous loss already...?"

I was now living entirely off the meager savings that were left after the sale of my condo. Following the earthquake, I found myself in a difficult economic situation. My insurance deductible was very high. In order to sell my condominium, I had to pay for the repairs, which were considerably less than the deductible. The only answer I had for my concerned critics was that I was trusting God's divine providence. But it was difficult to face all those doubts, however well-meant.

When Dr. Flaxie Fletcher, my dear friend and medical practitioner in California, posed those probing questions to me after my preflight medical examination in March 1995, I wept. "If I need transport, I will take the bus," I told her. "You know how much I love walking in Israel."

Then, in an effort to placate her, I added softly, "Listen, I've been fortunate to live in such a nice place. My condo is very charming and quaint. But what can I say, material things don't have the same priority in my life anymore. My sole purpose in life is prayer and studying the Word of God. You know all the barbecues I missed during the holidays, choosing to study the Bible instead. When I get involved with my studying, I can't put the books down until I find the answer.

"As I see it, the true riches are eternal. The satisfaction I receive from studying is a priceless commodity. It's intangible! You can't touch it with the human senses.

"You know how I've always wanted to live in Israel and study Torah in Hebrew. The entire Land of Israel is holy and I can feel the peace of the Almighty. I could choose the ways of the world or I could choose the way of God. I've chosen a rich spiritual heritage that gives me peace. The Jewish Sages said, 'Rich is he who is happy with his lot.' So you see, my dear, I am a wealthy person. You cannot purchase peace of mind; it's a rare commodity."

Others had asked me the same questions, but I hadn't cried. Later I wondered why I had wept when Flaxie asked them. Here lies the answer: The tears were not of sadness, but tears of joy. I realized that simultaneously I was both poor and rich. I knew Flaxie wouldn't understand, but at last I was beginning to. She had asked those valid questions as a concerned friend.

Finally, the day came, and I was on holy ground once again. All my old friends were back in America, and here in Israel I was faced with the dilemma of finding a place to live. I couldn't stay in a hotel forever. Rabbi Mordechai Goldberg kindly extended me an open invitation to stay with his family until I was able to get myself settled.

The morning I was due to check out of the hotel, I received a telephone call from his wife, Avigail.

"*Shalom*, Ahuvah. The children and I are delighted that you're going to be our guest for a while. Do you need help moving your luggage?"

"Yes, I planned to take a taxi."

"No, no, that's ridiculous," Avigail said. "I'll be over in fifteen minutes to pick you up."

Was there no end to the loving-kindness of this family? I had to sit down and ponder this thought: *How the Jewish people love converts – and I hadn't even started the process yet!* Then I thought about Ruth of the Bible. I wondered if she had experienced anything like this. I had read her story many times, but I had no clue as to how she felt during her struggles.

Avigail and I lugged my suitcase to her third-floor apartment. Regaining my breath at last, I asked Avigail if she knew where I should start looking for an apartment. She suggested that I check the bulletin board at their synagogue in Old Katamon and recommended a rental agency in town.

I paid my registration fee at the agency and requested a listing for Old Katamon, Mordechai and Avigail's neighborhood. It was the only one I was familiar with. After some discussion I asked about Bayit Vegan, the section where Yosef lived.

The agent looked up skeptically. "We very seldom get apartments in Bayit Vegan. Try again next week," she suggested. I followed her advice, but still nothing was listed for Bayit Vegan.

The first flat I saw in Old Katamon was shocking. In the United States, a respectable landlord couldn't show such a squalid apartment. However, I didn't expect instant results and braced myself for a long search. Being on the receiving end of hospitality wasn't easy for a veteran high-flying airline marketing executive, but I counseled myself to be patient.

Here one needed an enormous dose of *savlanut* (as they call patience in Israel) and constant prayer to prevent high blood pressure. When I first arrived in Israel there was nothing I missed about the United States, but the longer I was in Israel the more I started missing the professionalism and courtesy of the American people. The Middle East was a very different place!

Before I left California, Ruth had said, "Well, I guess you just choose your crazies! It's either earthquakes or suicide bombings." I was beginning to understand how things were culturally different in Israel. *Am I meshugah?* I sometimes wondered.

I loved praying at the Western Wall. I had started walking there (only a thirty-minute walk from Old Katamon) two afternoons a week to pray. I always sensed that the place was holy. Right from the very first time I prayed there, my prayer list all carefully written out, I knew that every prayer I prayed would be answered. In I Kings 8:41–43 I had read King Solomon's prayer at the dedication of the Temple: "When a stranger, not of Thy people, comes to the Temple to pray, God should hear and answer them." What an incredible experience! Aspiring to turn my life and will over to the Master of the World, I knew I was praying to the God that Jews throughout the centuries had prayed to for thousands of years. This thought brought tears to my eyes.

When my business was just getting off the ground and I was in Israel as a tour host, I'd take my group to the Wall. I'd find a separate space and pray for my plans to prosper. I tried to pray for everyone I knew, spontaneously and briefly. In my prayer, three requests were paramount: my family's well-being, good health, and that I would be able to live in Israel.

Here my prayers were answered. Thank God, I was now in Israel to stay. But where to stay? That was the problem.

One desperate day, my search for living quarters having continued for two months, I spilled my heart out at the Wall. Afterwards, I lingered at the awesome remnant of the Holy Temple for a long time. When I left, I thought perhaps I should call Yosef. Maybe he would have some words of encouragement.

Two days later when I returned from praying at the Wall again, Avigail told me, "Ahuvah, Yosef called. He wants you to call him. I understand that you are invited to stay in Bayit Vegan for Shabbos. I think you'll have a lovely time there. Do you know that it's *chareidi*?"

"Yes, Avigail. I feel very comfortable in a black neighborhood." We both laughed. In a *chareidi* neighborhood the majority of the men dress in black suits and hats. The word *chareidi* literally means God-fearing, but colloquially these people are often referred to as "black."

Rabbi Gabriel Beer, who would be hosting me, was Yosef's former teacher at a Hebrew school in Far Rockaway, New York. The Beers had moved to Bayit Vegan in 1969. It sounded like this Shabbos was going to be a very special one. Indeed, the warmth and peace in the Beers' home surpassed my expectations.

Chaya Beer came to the door to answer my knock. "*A gutten erev Shabbos*!" we greeted each other. I gave Mrs. Beer a bouquet of flowers as an expression of gratitude for hosting me. Rabbi Beer came and introduced himself.

Yosef had told my hosts that I was intending to convert. "I am looking forward to hearing more about your story during dinner," Rabbi Beer remarked.

Chaya and I lit candles and prayed *Kabbalas Shabbos*. Shortly afterwards Rabbi Beer and Yosef returned from synagogue. We had a lovely evening. Rabbi Beer told us stories about Torah sages and Yosef gave us a *devar Torah*. I was on the edge of my seat the whole time.

Upon finishing our meal, Rabbi Beer suggested that we go for a Shabbos walk. The Beers seemed to know everyone. They introduced me to several families while we were strolling. They were all incredibly friendly! I kept thinking to myself, *Oh, how I would love to live in this neighborhood. There's something very different about it.*

Rabbi Beer had spoken so highly of the Heymans at the Shabbos table that I got very excited when I was told they were approaching us. I saw a distinguished-looking, middle-aged couple coming toward us. I couldn't believe my eyes when I gazed at Rabbi Heyman. Light was radiating from his chin to his forehead. My imagination soared. I thought to myself, *Is that how Moses's face looked with the shining light of the Divine Presence, after he spoke to Hashem on Mount Sinai?*

I was in awe of their presence until Chaya introduced me to the them. Rabbi Heyman looked at me and said, "She has a special *neshamah*. I wish you success."

Chaya told me, "Ahuvah, he doesn't give out *berachos* so easily."

My first impression was that those people were holy. What I experienced during our Shabbos walk was the same peace I had experienced walking down the street on Yom Kippur. Instinctively, I felt at home.

Chaya and I went to pray at the Gra Synagogue at 7:00 the next morning. The only thing I could think of was that it was very early, especially since I had mulled over my first Shabbos in Bayit

Vegan for many hours during the night, getting little sleep. This was the first time I had been in an Ashkenazic *chareidi* synagogue. Even though I couldn't understand a word anyone was saying, I felt very comfortable.

Because I was curious, I spent a lot of time watching the men down below. Most were dressed in black and had the traditional tallis draped around them like a garment. The cantor had an angelic voice and his chanting in Hebrew moved me. My soul was rejoicing. I repeatedly thought to myself, *I've never seen anything like this in my life.*

When they took the Torah out of the Ark, the men took the ends of their talleisim, kissed the strings, and placed them on the Torah scroll. This scene brought tears to my eyes. *Oh, how they love God.*

The *rebbetzin* helped me follow the service in my siddur. When it was time to return the Torah to the ark, they sang the same words I had heard in Old Katamon. "*Eitz chaim hi lamachazikim bah, v'tomcheha meushar....* It [the Torah] is a tree of life for those who grasp it, and its supporters are praiseworthy. Its ways are ways of pleasantness and all its paths are peace." My soul seemed so connected to those words.

Chaya must have read my mind because she asked me after leaving the synagogue, "How did you enjoy the praying, Ahuvah?"

"I've never seen nor experienced anything like this in my entire life," I replied. "I will be so happy when I can understand Hebrew and follow the order of the service."

"It takes time, Ahuvah. It used to take me four hours to pray in Hebrew when I first started. Be patient and study hard; Hashem should help you."

It seemed that any words I chose to convey my feelings were grossly inadequate. How could I explain what my soul had just experienced. The thought of praying in Jerusalem, in such a holy place, gave me chills.

Before departing Rebbetzin Heyman asked me if I was enjoying their neighborhood and extended an invitation for me to return. It warmed my heart; I so wanted to come back.

I was to have Shabbos lunch with the Schwartzbaums. Avraham Schwartzbaum had written an amazing book called *The Bamboo Cradle* about the adoption of their child, a Chinese baby whom they had found abandoned at a railway station in Taiwan. With much difficulty, Avraham and his wife, Rochel, had succeeded in raising her as an Orthodox Jewess. That was why Yosef had said that the Schwartzbaums and I would be compatible. After finishing our lunch and hearing Dr. Schwartzbaum's lucid *devar Torah*, I thought, *What a lovely family! Yosef was right!*

When it was time for me to leave Bayit Vegan, I didn't want to go; I felt bonded to the families I had met. I knew this would not be my last visit. I also sensed that the synagogue called "the Gra" was just what I needed for my spiritual growth. Above all, I had found a neighborhood that felt like home.

That evening when I arrived back at the Goldbergs' after my memorable Shabbos in Bayit Vegan, Mordechai was sitting on the floor with Avigail strumming on his guitar. He asked me, "How are things in the 'hood'?" He had a fascination with people's roots and "deep-earth spirituality," as he called it.

He and Avigail introduced me to a friend, Faye Bliume, who was also into quoting *tehillim*. They felt they had made a heavenly match when, one afternoon a few days later, the two of us walked together to the Western Wall quoting psalms the entire way!

I doubt if Mordechai and Avigail will ever forget this period of their lives. I know that I won't. After I had moved in and asked where I would be sleeping, I learned that another friend was occupying the guest room with her daughter and a puppy. I told them I would stay elsewhere. But Avigail would have none of that; after all, who would make the Southern fried chicken and peach cobbler? So I stayed in the living room.

Still grieving the loss of my mother, I was no more in touch with my feelings than I had been two months before, when I arrived at the Goldbergs. But there was no question that the family environment was emotionally healthy for me. In fact, I'm sure it was the medicine that the doctor would have prescribed at that time in my life.

That Sunday morning after praying, I took a fresh look back at the events of the previous days. I concluded that there were no coincidences; it was just God's way of remaining anonymous! I knew it was meant to be that Ruth and I had met and started the Festival of Freedom. Nor was it coincidental that Yosef had read that article in the *Jerusalem Post* and started corresponding with Ruth. She had told me, "Ahuvah, I've started corresponding with the nicest man, and we're going to meet him soon." Later, it was Yosef who introduced me to the Goldbergs and my new friends in Bayit Vegan.

I was particularly impressed by the genuineness of the Jewish people and by their spiritual strength, so reminiscent of my own family's. The men seemed so meticulous in carrying out their religious obligations and the women were so dedicated to the welfare of their families. I remembered that Rabbi Beer had once said there was a fence around the Torah. That was it! The Jewish people have a Divine assignment, a mandate from

Hashem to guard and protect the Torah. Thanks to the protectors of the Torah a person like me could experience a rich spiritual inheritance. Otherwise, it would have been lost. That was so wonderful!

All of a sudden, Avigail walked into the room. "Ahuvah, are you talking to yourself again?"

"Yes, I seem to be doing this quite frequently," I said with a laugh. "They say it's okay, as long as you don't answer yourself."

Avigail, Yosef, and I arranged to meet together for lunch at Alumah's Restaurant later that day. Yosef asked me if I had enjoyed Shabbos. "It was one of the nicest Shabbosos I've ever had," I said, "especially since there's no traffic in Bayit Vegan." Then it clicked. "That's it!"

Yosef was perplexed. "Ahuvah, would you please explain what you're talking about?"

"What I mean is, I've never been in a neighborhood before where there's no traffic on Shabbos, where everyone goes to synagogue. You can actually wake up and hear the praying. The place is holy. I've never experienced anything like this before in my life. I didn't even know that such a place existed." By now the volume of my voice was about ten decibels and two octaves above normal.

Yosef smiled. "I am delighted that my neighborhood has had such a profound effect on you."

"That's it. I have finally figured it out. When you get a group of people who are holy and who believe that God is holy and whose every heartbeat is to sanctify God's Name, then the place is holy. They function in unity. These people are holy. You know, I've never experienced anything like the spiritual power of the Jewish people."

"Ahuvah, the Jewish people have a covenant with God, to

sanctify His Name through the study of Torah and the six hundred and thirteen commandments." I nodded eagerly, having heard this before. "Thank God that the Jewish people preserved such a rich spiritual heritage, so that a person like me could be given an opportunity to tap into it!"

"Ahuvah, we have a tradition that Hashem offered the Torah to the other nations, but they refused. However, there were souls among those nations who wanted to accept the Torah. These are the souls of converts."

By now I was in tears. "Now I know why I made it here. Thank you, Yosef. You have just said the most beautiful words, which are the culmination of a lifetime search."

"It's okay, Ahuvah," Yosef continued. "Just know that Hashem loves the convert and so do the Jewish people. Let's order some lunch. I'm starving."

"I don't know if I have much of an appetite now. I think I need to digest the spiritual food first. I'll just order a soup and carrot juice."

While Yosef and Avigail were placing their orders, I pulled out the computerized listing of vacant apartments. I stared at one entry, astounded.

"Look, you won't believe it. There's an apartment listed in Bayit Vegan." I must have added another ten decibels, because I noticed people were watching. However, I was so excited I didn't care.

"Avigail, may I use your cell phone.... Oh, can you please take the telephone. He doesn't speak English."

After a lengthy conversation with the owner Yosef said, "Ahuvah, it's on a lovely quiet street, Weisburg. There's only one thing, though — the rent is five hundred dollars a month. Can you afford that?"

"Yes. Tell him I'd like to see it today." By now, I was having heart palpitations.

I couldn't believe it. Was I dreaming? The first Sunday after spending that lovely Shabbos in Bayit Vegan and already an apartment was available.

While we were waiting for lunch, even Yosef was starting to get excited. That was the first time I had ever seen him so animated. "Ahuvah, that's great! I tell you, I think that Hashem is watching out for you. If this works out, you couldn't be in a finer neighborhood."

Because my Hebrew was limited, Yosef offered to do the negotiating. When Mr. Amiton, the owner, took us into the living room, I could only think about how gorgeous the place was and how lovely my furniture would look there. I took in the breathtaking view from the living room window while the two men conversed in Hebrew. I was thrilled with the bedroom, which had lots of room for my books.

When we were out of hearing range, Yosef said, "Ahuvah, if he offers you the apartment for four hundred and fifty to four hundred and seventy-five dollars a month, take it. It's a beautiful flat for that price. All you have to do is move in, it's so clean."

I was so excited that when I left Yosef to catch the bus back to Old Katamon, I went to the wrong bus stop. Yosef happened to look back and yelled, "Ahuvah, you need to catch Bus 24 across the street, remember?"

I was so nervous I didn't know what I was doing! With my first apartment in Jerusalem in Bayit Vegan, I thought that I had died and gone to Heaven! To me, Bayit Vegan was like heaven on earth!

My emotions were running high. The next day, I called Mr. Amiton at 11:00 P.M. "*Tov*, Miss Gray, Ruth and I are very happy to have you as a tenant." I only had to sign the lease and I would have my feet planted firmly on the ground of Eretz Yisrael!

On Thursday morning, when I was due to pick up the keys, I realized that I didn't have a bed. I decided to call Chaya Beer. When she heard that I was moving to Bayit Vegan, Chaya answered elatedly, "You should be *gebenched*! Oh, don't worry, Ahuvah. We have a cot that we can lend you. Do you need linens as well?"

Chaya's son Eli came with the bed and linen. I was so impressed with the love and support that was being extended to me. I thought of my mother. *I must be receiving all this kindness because of her deeds*, I mused. Otherwise, I was unable to explain it.

Food hadn't even crossed my mind, but it was close to dinnertime and I was beginning to feel hunger pangs. Then I remembered I hadn't called Rochel Schwartzbaum. I knew she would be ecstatic that I was living in the neighborhood.

Immediately, she said, "Ahuvah, don't buy anything. I have plenty of food. I was just warming something up for us. I'll just finish this up, and I'll be right over. Do you have a refrigerator and a stove?"

"No, I don't. Thanks for reminding me. I'll have to purchase them." We both started laughing.

Within twenty minutes, Rochel appeared at my door with what I called "gourmet delight on wheels." She had prepared a wonderful stir-fry vegetable with chicken and a salad. For dessert, I had pound cake. There was so much food, there was even enough for breakfast. The thermos canister with the dry ice was a great idea.

I gave Rochel a tour of the apartment. "Ahuvah, this is so lovely. What a great view."

When Rochel was about to leave, she turned and looked at

the food on the table. Then she said, "Ahuvah, do you have a chair?"

"No, I don't. Good you asked. I hadn't even realized it. But with a great meal like this, I can stand up and still enjoy it."

"No, no, Ahuvah. I'll go get a chair." She was so insistent, I could do nothing to stop her. "I'll be right back," she said as she left.

Ten minutes later, she returned with a yellow chair. I thanked her again for everything and set the table for my gourmet dinner.

Before I went to bed that night, I thanked God for all of His blessings. I was still overwhelmed by all the kindness and support I had received. I thought perhaps this was all a dream. If so, I hoped it would never end! Bayit Vegan was indeed unique. I could never recall anyone offering me any kind of support or assistance when I had moved into new places in the States. To calm myself, I sat in bed and read a few psalms from my Bible. I remember closing my eyes as I recited Psalm 24: "Hashem's is the earth and its fullness, the inhabited land and those who dwell in it." Quietly, I whispered, "I am living in Jerusalem."

The next day, Yosef introduced me to the butcher, Moshe Rosenbaum. I didn't know when I first met the Rosenbaum family that I would be spending numerous Shabbosos with them.

Afterwards, I contemplated what a lovely neighborhood I had chosen. Everyone was so friendly and accepting. I was introduced to Rabbi Zev Gotthold, whom another rabbi had recommended for assisting with my conversion. Rabbi Gotthold coached me entirely as an act of *chesed*. I felt very privileged indeed to be under the tutelage of such a well-qualified person. Until 1975, Rabbi Gotthold was a director in the Department for Contact with the Diaspora, under the Israel Ministry for Religious Affairs. Now employed in a volunteer capacity, he assisted the Rabbinate in dealing with conversion applications.

Over and over again, I thanked God for Rabbi Gotthold. To me, the rabbi was a spiritual mentor and I agreed wholeheartedly with all he suggested. His great sense of humor reminded me of my father.

"Ahuvah," the rabbi told me one day, "I have two women in Bayit Vegan who have volunteered to teach you. Here are their names and telephone numbers." As I took the piece of paper, I couldn't hold back the tears in my eyes. "I am sure you'll find them capable teachers," he continued.

"Rabbi Gotthold, I don't know how I can thank you!"

"For what? Just study hard, Ahuvah, so we can get this done quickly."

I had already met Malka Jacobson, who sat next to me in shul and assisted me with the order of prayer in my siddur. Her sister-in-law, Esther Jacobson, Rabbi Gotthold's cousin, tutored me in Chumash. I became quite fond of both women, who were very warm and devoted. We had a weekly schedule for learning Torah and prayer. Even though the few hours per week were much less than what I needed and wanted, they added a new dimension to my life. I used to count the hours remaining until my next session.

Knowledge of halachah, kashrus, the Jewish calendar, holidays, prayer, Jewish history, and Tanach commentaries was required for conversion. I could see that I had a lot of ground to cover before being ready for the mikveh. I had moved to Jerusalem in order to live in the Holy City and study Torah, so I was very disappointed to find that the seminaries were not primarily organized for prospective converts. However, I was determined to find a seminary that would accept me.

Learning Hebrew, though, was by far my greatest challenge; my hobbling efforts were frustrating and always humbling. I met Americans who had lived in Israel for fifteen years and still didn't know Hebrew. I hadn't studied any language since high school. With my whole experience in languages comprising two years of French at school, plus learning classical Greek at the Total Word Concept Institute, I didn't feel I was gifted in linguistics. My social network was almost entirely English speaking and all of my efforts seemed to be only a drop in the bucket compared to what was needed.

All that time, I was still praying three times a day and going to synagogue on Shabbos. There were days when I felt that my head would explode! Then I would recall my mother's trait of perseverance. I said to myself, *Surely, if my mother worked at her job for forty-two years, I can learn Hebrew and retain all these grammar rules and new expressions.*

Sure enough, I gained instant strength!

In time, my one-bedroom apartment became established as my new home. My family members in the States were elated that I had a permanent telephone number where they could reach me. Before leaving the States I had packed only what was needed to start up a household. Now, I could call the shipping company in the States and told them to send my lift. In retrospect, I wouldn't recommend moving to a foreign country the way I did. What a way to move! No furniture or appliances – just my clothes and a few of my favorite books. But not knowing any better, I did it my way!

Chapter 8

Lech Lecha

August 29, 1995. It was 4:30 A.M. when the telephone rang. Anxiously, I grabbed the receiver. Who could be calling at such an hour? I heard my sister Nellie's voice. "Hello, Lobo, you won't believe this. Ezra Junior had a massive heart attack. The doctors don't expect him to live."

My heart was pulsating violently, but I managed to remain calm. My mother had passed away only eight months before. "Nellie, I don't care what the doctors say, Ezra is not going to die. We'll just have to believe that God will work a miracle."

"Lobo, his main artery split! We all need to get together and pray." Before I hung up the telephone, my sister said, "Let's continue with our family tradition and fast, too. Will you go to the Wailing Wall to pray?"

"Yes, I think that's a good idea." Nellie and I synchronized our watches for the fast.

As I hung up the telephone, Rabbi Emanuel Feldman's words reverberated through my head. "Ahuvah, you are doing a very courageous thing." That's what he said when he heard of my converting to Judaism. Until that phone call, I had not fully understood the ramifications of his statement. Here I was, six thousand miles away from my family while they were going through such a crisis. What could I do? The only thing to do was to say a spontaneous prayer. "Our Father, I pray to the God of the Patriarchs. Lord, as a family we've been through a lot. We have just lost our mother. However, if it is Your will for my brother to die, who am I to question God, for he is Your child. You formed him in my mother's womb. I release Ezra into Your care."

Sleep was out of the question and I recited psalms until dawn. Then I headed for the Western Wall, tense and filled with anxiety. As I walked into the Old City my anxiety dissipated. I again experienced that wonderful secure feeling that Hashem would hear my prayers in that holy place.

I spent the entire day praying and reading the Scriptures, which helped me fast. I was sure that Nellie had called our father and Oscar because she always took care of such details. The important thing was to keep praying.

My thoughts often wandered back to my roots. Even though I was getting to know some wonderful families, I really missed my own. There wasn't a day that I didn't think about my mother. After her death, there was a bonding between my siblings and me. We had been close before, but we became even closer with her passing. On such occasions, we remembered our mother's wisdom and uncanny foresight. She had told us, "One day, you're going to be proud of one another and depend on each other. You've got to learn to get along." I felt that our mother would have been very proud of us if she had been with us through that crisis.

Three days later Nellie called again. "Lobo, did you go to the Western Wall?"

"Yes, I have been going there every day."

"Well, Lobo, I believe that Ezra's going to live."

"Nellie, are you serious? I can't believe it."

"So do I. I'm sure Ezra will get better now. Let's just continue praying."

Nellie finally had a chance to tell me about all that had transpired in the days before her phone call. Ezra had been feeling violently ill. Despite everyone's desperate pleading, he refused to go to the hospital. Finally, after more than two hours of fruitless coaxing by his anxious family, he passed out. He was sent by ambulance to intensive care for emergency surgery which lasted for twelve hours. When it was over, the doctors told us that he had a burst blood vessel and they didn't expect him to live.

On her next call, Nellie exclaimed, "Hello, Lobo! You won't believe it; it's a miracle. Nobody can explain it! Not the nurses, not even the doctors. Ezra is sitting up in bed laughing and talking and drinking Pepsi Cola."

"Thank God!" I sighed. "Have you spoken to him?"

"Yes. He seems to be alert and stable." I could hear the relief in my sister's voice.

"Very good. Please give me the number at the hospital."

When I heard my brother's voice, I couldn't believe it. He sounded great. We shared a few jokes and I talked to his wife and my niece and nephew.

A miracle it certainly was! Six times Ezra had come under what they call "code blue," with emergency personnel called in to revive him. My brother had been wavering between life and death while I was praying *minchah*, the afternoon prayer, at the Western Wall.

After another three long and fatiguing days, I was awakened once more at 4:30 in the morning. "Hello, Lobo. I am sorry to call you so early in the morning, but it's another problem with Ezra.

He has gone into cardiac arrest and I'm afraid the doctors are not optimistic."

When my sister lapsed into silence, I quoted *Tehillim*. "Whoever sits in the refuge of the Most High, he shall dwell in the protective shade of the Almighty" (91:1). "Nellie, I'll continue to pray at the Wall. He's not going to die. I don't care what it looks like. When are you going to Chicago?"

"Tomorrow morning. Do you think we should fast again?"

"Yes. Call me when you get there." Before I hung up the phone, we synchronized our watches for another fast. I found myself reeling under the new blow. I had no strength left. The strain of being separated from my family, studying Hebrew, studying for a conversion, changing my religion, and now facing my brother's terrifying condition had worn me down. There was only one thing to do now. Pray.

I sat down in the living room and gazed at the panoramic view of Gilo and Bethlehem. "Dear God," I said softly, "I really don't understand any of this." This was not a time to fall apart and I knew it was essential that I stayed focused during the crisis. I didn't make any demands of God. It wasn't like making a shopping list. I took my Tanach and held it close, as I usually did in difficult times. I then said a very brief prayer: "Lord, let Your will be done." As soon as daylight came, I got dressed and went to the Wall to pray.

Upon Nellie's arrival in Chicago, she set up residence at the hospital. She never left my brother's bedside, deeming the nursing care inadequate. She set a clock to wake her up every half-hour during the night so she could turn Ezra to prevent him from developing bedsores. We were in constant contact — at least two or three times a day.

Ezra underwent a second operation. I prayed with every ounce of my remaining strength that all of Ezra's blood vessels would function properly during the procedure. I felt a sense of relief knowing that I was offering the best of my service in prayer.

Slowly Ezra started to recuperate. I continued to pray. Every time I talked to my sister, she asked, "Have you been to the Western Wall?" It was amazing to me that my sister, who had never been to Israel, knew all about the "Wall." Perhaps she had seen pictures of men praying there. It was so fascinating that my family knew the benefit of my praying and especially at that holy place. What a privilege, I thought, to be living in Jerusalem and getting prayer requests from America! No matter which religion they belonged to, people seemed to value the significance of praying at the Wall.

Ezra recovered gradually; he was hospitalized for about a month and a half. Nellie was with him the entire time. Ezra's brain had been deprived of oxygen from the heart attack and he had difficulty with his short-term memory. (His long-term memory, thank God, had not been affected.) The most painful experience was when he didn't remember that Rennie and Mother had passed away. Eventually my sister had to tell him because he kept asking for them.

Whenever I phoned Ezra at home, he would ask, "Don't you miss us?"

"Yes, Ezra, I miss you very much. However, I've chosen a new life, and I'm trying to adjust to a different culture, a new language."

"How are your studies progressing?"

"Very well. My biggest difficulty is learning Hebrew."

"You're very intelligent, I know you'll do well."

With time, I realized that everyone was adjusting to my being in Jerusalem. It was so precious to still have the support of my family, who had always supported me in all my endeavors in life. After hearing horrendous stories from converts who had no contact with their families, I prayed to God, "Hashem, please help my family to understand." It would have been unbearable to think of losing them.

Whenever Nellie heard or saw any violence on the news, she always called to check on me.

"Nellie," I said soothingly, "I can assure you that I am fine; I wasn't even aware of any shooting on the Lebanese border. We're so far away from there. Besides, my neighborhood is very peaceful. You would love it."

My sister would interject lovingly, "You can always come home."

In a very soft voice I would respond, "Nellie, I am at home. Israel is my home now."

I later told the story of our family crisis to Rabbi and Rebbetzin Aaron Feldman over their Shabbos table. Rabbi Feldman said, "Ahuvah, you come from an amazing family."

I smiled. "Rabbi Feldman, I think so, too."

When I shared my story with the Beers, Rabbi Beer said, "Ahuvah, your sister is a *tzadeikes*."

Indeed, I believe Nellie is deserving of the title. One Sunday, long before I made aliyah to Israel, I visited Nellie's place of worship and heard her make a strong appeal for volunteers to assist with her "Lunch Bag Ministry," a project to feed the homeless. I was eager to help because she had always helped me when I needed her good resolve and sound reasoning. The following day I made a few telephone calls and discovered that B'nai B'rith (a

Jewish community organization) donated food to the needy. To collect the food, all I had to do was bring a letter from Nellie's pastor.

Every week I'd pick up the food from the contact person, Dave, in the San Fernando Valley and then deliver it to Nellie in Beverly Hills. The food we received was different every week. Sometimes Dave gave me an assortment of fruits, potato chips, and crackers. Other times he gave me canned goods. Then he gave me the name and telephone number of a meat company in the San Fernando Valley that donated deli beyond its freshness date. (It wasn't spoiled, but it couldn't be sold.) All I had to do was pick it up.

Eventually, I started preparing the sandwiches and then went with Nellie to downtown Los Angeles, where we distributed the bags of food to the homeless. What a humbling experience it was! The homeless people were already lined up when we arrived. They weren't all derelicts. There were all kinds of needy people — elderly men and women, youths, and little children, some healthy, some ill. After conversing with a few, I discovered that each individual had a unique story. One fellow was a lawyer. His wife had left him and he had given up all hope of ever being a decent human being again. Due to Nellie's diligent efforts, he eventually pulled himself together and became a success story.

Every other Sunday my sister, accompanied by two friends, drove the skid-row people to their place of worship. Afterwards, she brought them home for supper. Some Sundays after services, we called our mother to share our activities with her. I remember how excited Nellie was and how she exclaimed, "Mother, you remember Bob, the one that was a lawyer and his wife left him. Well, he's not drinking anymore. He comes to service every

Sunday. He's found a job and he's going to visit his wife and daughter in San Francisco."

Mother blessed her, "Nellie, this is great work that you're doing. May the Lord continue to strengthen you. Delores, you continue to help your sister, okay?"

"Yes, Mother. I am doing all I can."

I couldn't express in words the wonderful feeling I had when I realized that my sister and I were emulating our mother and grandmother. It was well worth all the effort and time we put into it. I can truly say that that Lunch Bag Ministry opened a new world for Nellie.

She soon informed me that her house of prayer was working on a new project, feeding the homeless on Thanksgiving. As usual, Nellie was heading the project. I asked if there was anything I could do to help. She said, "No, you're too busy with your own projects, but you can show up to help feed them."

All too soon, Thanksgiving Day arrived. I couldn't believe my eyes when I got to the distribution point. People were lined up for blocks: men, women, entire families. Chefs had cooked the turkeys with cornbread stuffing. There was green beans and candied yams, corn on the cob and salads galore. I'd never seen so much food in one place before. Finally I saw Nellie with a cell phone; she was coordinating the entire operation. I gave her a hug and a kiss and told her it was all so remarkable. She responded that she had had only two hours of sleep the night before.

I told her she should go home immediately and get some rest. "That's impossible," she said. "Who's going to coordinate everything?"

I knew arguing would be futile, so I asked what I should do. She told me, "Go to the room where the clothes are and help them organize the clothes and shoes to give away." Then she turned to speak to the doctors who had just arrived.

I marveled at how she had thought of everything. The homeless had gotten a complete overhaul: A good wholesome meal, clothing, even medical care. Nellie had personally called up doctors and hospitals to request their involvement. Fortunately, a new free service, "Ask the Doctor," offered to help, while two of the biggest hospitals in L. A., Cedar Sinai and St. John's, volunteered their staff. There were doctors cleaning sores and giving flu shots! B'nai B'rith had donated blankets. Volunteers had left their families to serve food to the needy on Thanksgiving Day.

What a way to live out the American dream! No job was too humbling; some volunteers even washed the feet of the homeless. We all had one thing in common: we came to serve. I watched and participated with tears in my eyes, seeing the loving concern for our fellow man, with no regard for color or creed.

I was there for hours, first distributing clothing and then helping to serve the food, until a girl came over and asked, "Are you Nellie's sister?" I nodded. "Nellie said you should go to her home and start cooking dinner there. She left the turkey out, and the celery, onions, and green pepper are already chopped up for the dressing."

I drove straight down Santa Monica to my sister's place in Beverly Hills. When my sister came home, she looked utterly exhausted, but I was so proud of her. Our meal, served at 8:30 that night, tasted better than ever before because we knew that we had helped so many people enjoy theirs. I knew that Nellie would tell my mother just how many people were there and how next year she would work to have more volunteers, influencing more places and involving more people. I knew my parents were very proud of the work that Nellie was doing. So was I.

Nellie's Lunch Bag Ministry continues to thrive today. She has managed to remain constantly dedicated to such projects for the best part of twenty years, in addition to running a freelance graphic business. Nellie, who covets no honor, explains: "Giving to the community is the only way to honor my mother and do what she taught me to do."

I have memories from my childhood of my mother often coming home from work with a stranger or two. "Make yourself at home!" she'd tell them, introducing us. Then she'd disappear into the kitchen to start dinner. Even as a six-year-old, I noticed that the guests were dressed rather strangely, and were shaggy-haired and unshaven. But what did that matter? They were guests and they seemed like very nice people.

It's hard to believe today that Nellie was the one who once asked our mother, "Why are these people sitting at the table with us? Why don't they take a bath? They smell!"

We waited for Mother's answer – she always had the answers – but she just gave Nellie a look that spoke louder than anything she could have said. It was from my mother that I learned how powerful and expressive silence can be.

"Won't you please help yourselves to another helping of roast and potatoes?" my mother asked our guests, smiling sweetly and serenely.

After our guests had left, my mother explained, "They're bums. They live on skid row and they don't have a home to take a bath in."

When Nellie and I joined together to feed the homeless, it reminded me of the goodness of God in feeding all of mankind and of the Patriarch Abraham's kindness to strangers, as he emulated his Creator. Years later, in a Jerusalem seminary, I learned that Avraham, after his circumcision, had prayed to Hashem for guests. God had increased the sun's heat to spare Avraham that physical strain, since no normal person would venture out of doors on such a hot afternoon. But when Avraham did see three travelers he ran toward them, ignoring his great pain. How unique he was and how worthy to become the spiritual father of all mankind! I wept when I learned that because Avraham so reminded me of my mother and sister's acts of kindness.

I also learned that Avraham established an inn (*eshel*) in Be'er Sheva. All wayfarers that passed by were fed and given shelter for the night. Whenever I learned anything about Avraham, I always felt in awe of the great patriarch.

I left Israel in December 1995 to visit my family and see my brother alive with my very own eyes. It was a year since I had last seen my family, and I had already started the conversion process in Jerusalem. Because I planned to stay in America for two months, I gave up my lovely apartment in Bayit Vegan and looked forward to studying in a seminary on my return.

Daddy met me at the airport, and we exchanged a warm hug and kiss. True to his nature, he started crying.

"Daddy, why are you crying?" I asked.

He didn't answer me, just continued to cry like Granddaddy, may he rest in peace, had. Every summer when I went to visit my grandparents, my grandfather would cry when I arrived and when I left.

The ride from O'Hare Airport to my brother's home in Hyde Park afforded me a rare opportunity to enjoy my father's company.

My father soon brought the conversation around to my

mother. "Delores, I still can't believe that Chris is dead. You know, I always loved your mother. And she was so beautiful! Did she ever tell you about the time I visited her in the hospital after she had had the stroke and brought her two dozen red roses?"

"Yes, Daddy, she told me. She said you apologized for everything that had happened between you and that you cried like a baby."

"It's true, I sure did, girl. I couldn't stop crying."

How precious those moments were! I reflected on how seldom the two of us had been able to share our inner feelings, as we were doing then.

"Being without Mom is difficult for me, too. But I don't miss her nearly as much in Jerusalem as I do when I am in the States. In Jerusalem, I feel like she's with me everywhere I go. My life has become so rich and complete since I moved to Israel."

"You seem to be very happy every time we speak. Do you think you'll get married again, honey?"

"I pray that some time in the distant future, I will. But I have so much to learn about being a Jew. It isn't easy, I suppose, especially not for a Black Jew!" We looked at each other and laughed.

I was so anxious to see Ezra and his family! Seeing Ezra, however, proved to be another shocking experience. He had just been released from his marathon term in the hospital, and the man I remembered as assertive and successful in business was now stooped over a walker. The two of us hugged, and then I embraced his wife, Paula, their ten-year-old son, Frankie, and their eight-year-old daughter, Christina.

"Am I glad to see you alive and kicking," Ezra exclaimed. "Every time I asked Nellie about someone, she said that they were dead. Finally I asked, 'Is there anyone in our family still alive?'"

We all laughed. In life's tough situations, when you think you've come to the end of the road, you just have to keep smiling.

My brother and his family were celebrating their holiday season at the time of my visit. When it was time for me to light my Chanukah candles, Christina and Frankie were overjoyed. "Oh, Auntie Lobo has Chanukah candles!"

After reciting the traditional blessing for the lighting, I asked the children if they knew why the Jewish people lit candles. I told them all about the miracles that took place in the days of the Maccabees. They had already known from their parents that their Auntie Lobo lived in Israel and was studying to become Jewish. Their faces were all eyes and their mouths were full of questions. I was so pleased that I had remembered to bring my slides with me and could show them all the beautiful sights in Israel.

Chapter 9

"Harvard" Conversion

I'd like to preface this chapter by stating that out of my experiences, I have developed a deep love and respect for the institution of the beis din, and in particular, the personnel of the Jerusalem Beis Din. In retrospect, I am grateful for all of my experiences, no matter how arduous the journey along the way.

During my stay in the United States, I began to feel as if I could hardly breathe. It was as if I were suffocating! It wasn't the L. A. smog that was the problem; the morally polluted lifestyle reminded me of Sedom and Amorah. The dichotomy I was experiencing could be summed up in three succinct words: materialism versus spirituality. *Thank God for the religious Jews who have the stamina to live in America!* I thought. *Someone has to be a light unto the nations.*

Ruth was thrilled to have me back in California, even though I spent every Shabbos with observant Jewish families. However, it was the close contact I maintained with my friends in Israel that gave me the strength to remain in the States. What I thought would be a two-month trip turned into seven months. After half a year in my old environment, I was literally becoming ill. I was homesick for Jerusalem.

One morning after praying, I picked up my calendar, chose a date on which to leave, and told Pnina, the travel agent who'd taken over ticketing and booking my groups, to book my flight.

She answered, "Ahuvah, we still have work to do. There's pending group business yet to finalize."

I looked her in the eye and said, "I am leaving in August because I need to go home. I'll leave you a list of all pending groups. I can still follow up on some of them from Israel." I had earned enough money during my stay in California to carry me through the following December. The money would just have to last like the Chanukah miracle, when one small cruse of oil in the Holy Temple burned for eight days.

One morning I called Yosef to inform him of my return flight. Excitedly, he shared a Torah thought from the *Mishneh Torah*. "The Rambam mentions how the tribe of Levi was dedicated to studying and teaching Torah and therefore received financial and practical help from the people in the form of special tithes and gifts. Then he adds that just as the tribe of Levi merited support and help in its spiritual work, so will every person who separates himself from the vanities and emptiness of this world merit help.

"If this is true of every person," Yosef continued, "then it certainly should be true with someone who desires to join the Jewish people." Now he moved to the practical realm. "With this insight, Ahuvah, I began to pray that Hashem would find a place for you to live and study. After the prayer I made a few phone calls and found a seminary willing to accept you before your conversion."

"Yosef! How can I ever thank you? May you and all the people who have assisted me along my tedious journey receive a special *zechus* from the Almighty."

"Amen!" he responded. "The seminary is mailing you an application. The advantage that you have with this seminary is that it is in Bayit Vegan, and they have a dorm — this will solve your dilemma with housing. Ahuvah! Are you still there?"

"Yes," I answered, so overcome that I could hardly speak. At last my prayers had been answered. "Yosef, you're brilliant."

"It wasn't me, Ahuvah. It's all *min haShamayim*."

My sister was accustomed to my lengthy telephone calls to Israel by now. As soon as I got off the telephone, she wanted to know all the details. "Are you going to be living in a dorm? At least we don't have to worry anymore about how to contact you." She sighed.

Although I knew how hard my departure would be on my family, I couldn't wait to go home. Here I was in the country of my birth, and yet my soul longed for the *kedushah* of Eretz Israel. I went to bed with sweet dreams of returning.

The next day the application form arrived. I faxed it with a cover letter; two days later, I had a return fax stating that I was accepted to the Jerusalem seminary Nishmat, with dorm accommodations. Exhilarated, I started packing in haste; at last I had a home again! "Free at last, free at last, thank God Almighty, I am free at last."

My heart was filled with excitement, I anticipated how learning in a seminary would enhance my life. I had come a long way since the day when Avigail and I trudged upstairs with my luggage in Old Katamon. Soon I would be on the familiar tarmac of JFK, and back on my journey of faith.

As I fastened my seat belt and felt the familiar roar of the engines, I began to muse upon another road that I was still traveling

— the inexplicably frustrating journey of my conversion. My mind wandered back to a dear friend in Har Nof, who'd started her conversion process in Holland. There, her rabbi recommended that she go to Israel and complete her eighteen months of studies there.

"In Holland it takes seven years to convert," she said, "but here in Jerusalem, all they asked me to do was read Psalm 136 in Hebrew." That was one of my favorite psalms, and I had already mastered it in fluent Hebrew! "When I finished," she continued, "they said I definitely had a Jewish *neshamah*. That was it! I passed."[1]

"That was it?"

"Yes. That was it."

"But didn't they ask you where you lived prior to moving to Israel?"

"No."

"Didn't they ask you anything about your family?"

"No."

"Didn't they ask how many sisters and brothers you had?"

"No."

"They didn't ask you what your parents' professions were?"

"No."

---

1 This account is not in any way to be regarded as a standard procedure of any conversion court. "When approached by a prospective convert, a court must examine his case history and ascertain his true motives.... Acceptance of the yoke of the commandments is a very demanding undertaking, and the court must ascertain whether the candidate can sincerely and truly execute his commitment" (Schwartz, Rabbi Yoel, Jewish Conversion. Bayit Vegan, Jerusalem: The Kest-Lebovits Jewish Heritage and Roots Library, 1994, p. 31).

"Did they turn you down three times?"

"No."

I was stunned.

She must have seen the shock on my face. She explained that she had lived in the northern Galilee of Israel, and been turned down twice by the *beis din* there. The judges there did ask her about her family and background. Moreover, she had to have a friend write a letter verifying that she was committed to living by the 613 mitzvos. Still, compared to what I was going through, her conversion had been a simple affair.

As we reached cruising attitude, I closed my eyes and reviewed the milestones I'd passed on the long road to conversion. Shortly after I had finished the third annual Festival of Freedom, I was taken to the Ministry of the Interior by Sheefra Yakir, a friend of mine who'd converted twenty-three years before and was fluent in Hebrew. Before going to the Beis Din, I had to renew my visa.

When we arrived in the room, I couldn't believe my eyes! What a *balagan*. The place was full of people. Every seat was taken. The clerks behind the cubicles were yelling out numbers. The noise was unbelievable. We had to take a number and wait.

I looked at Sheefra and asked, "Are we going to be here all day?"

A short distance away from us sat an angry-looking man and a tearful woman. I pointed them out to Sheefra. "That couple is getting a divorce, and he wants custody of the children," she told me. "I know them well."

"Oh! No wonder that poor woman is crying."

Sheefra went over to speak to her friend, and I sat and tried to read a book. With all the distractions, it was impossible. One hour later, my number was called. Sheefra conversed with the clerk in Hebrew. I was asked to fill out a form and write a letter in Hebrew explaining why I wanted to convert in order for my tourist visa to be extended.

When Sheefra and I left the Interior Ministry, I didn't want to ever see the place again. "What a saga!" I said to Sheefra.

She laughed. "If you think that's difficult, wait till you go before the Beis Din!"

"Is it worse than what we have just experienced? I don't think I could have made it through this episode without your help."

"After my first visit to Beis Din, I wondered if I would make it through alive!" Sheefra retorted.

When the Hebrew letter from the Rabbinate arrived, I decided to call Rabbi Mordechai. He immediately volunteered to accompany me to the Beis Din and write a character reference. The hearing was scheduled for 10:00 on July 17, 1995. I davened with as much *kavanah* as possible that morning. Oh, how I wished Ruth could have been here with me! I needed her support. She had always been available when I needed her. "Two Women, One Journey," we called ourselves. However, my intuition told me that it was going to be a long journey before I joined the Jewish people.

As I walked through the door of the Beis Din, I thought of my mother. Her words rang in my ears: "Whatever you do in life, do it with dignity." I squared my shoulders and walked in as if I was the owner of the place.

The hallways were buzzing with Hebrew conversation. I walked into the room, sat down, and started reciting *Tehillim*. Moments later, a woman walked over to me and said, "Are you here for a conversion? Do you need help?"

I was astonished. She was an answer to my prayer.

"My name is Miri. What's yours?"

"I am Ahuvah. Pleased to meet you, Miri."

"It's nice to meet you, as well. Is this your first time here?"

"Yes."

"Are you nervous?"

"A little."

"The first time, these things don't go very well. They have to turn you away. Please don't take it personally. Do you speak any Hebrew?"

"Very little. I can understand a bit more than I can speak."

"Don't worry. I'll translate for you. Do you have a rabbi?"

"Yes. His name is Rabbi Mordechai Goldberg. He's meeting me here." I nervously looked at my watch. *Mordechai, oh, Mordechai, where are you?* I asked Miri if I should go and call him. I phoned the Goldbergs' home, but there was no answer. I went back to the room. Miri was still there. I told her that my rabbi must be on his way.

"Perhaps he's stuck in traffic."

"No, I believe he's on his bicycle." Miri looked at me and we both laughed.

Moments later the clerk called out my birth name: "Delores Gray." I looked around for Rabbi Mordechai once more. I was beginning to feel extremely nervous. Something must have happened! I wondered if something was wrong with one of the children. Miri and I walked through the door together.

As soon as we entered the room, my nervousness dissipated. This was so exciting! I'd never seen a Beis Din before. It looked just like a courtroom. There was a podium, on which we stood.

The three judges were seated on a platform. They had long white beards and were dressed in black. When they saw me, they looked at each other as if to say, "*Mah pitom?*"

The chief rabbi started to question me in Hebrew. Miri quickly came to my rescue. He and Miri engaged in intense dialogue. I could sense the gravity of their discussion and surmised that things weren't going in my favor.

As I stood there, I thought to myself, *Oh my goodness, they're gorgeous!* I meant in a religious sense. Here I was standing in a Jewish court at a pivotal point in my life. Then I smiled and thought, *As long as I am here, I might as well enjoy myself. Let's see, maybe the one in the middle looks a lot like Avraham. Perhaps the one on the left looks like Yitzchak, and the one on the right probably resembles Yaakov.*

The voice of the rabbi sitting in front shocked me back into reality. "*At midaberet Ivrit?* (Do you speak Hebrew?)"

"*K'tzat* (a little)," I responded.

They continued speaking with Miri. After about three minutes, Miri gestured to me to leave. As we turned away, one of the rabbis said, in perfect English, "Come back when you can speak Hebrew."

"But that could be never!" I retorted.

Miri told me not to take it personally. She took me to a bench and sat me down. "Ahuvah, please wait here. I'll be right back." I sat misty-eyed; never in my entire life had I felt so rejected. I wanted to cry, but I couldn't.

Miri came back. She said kindly, "Ahuvah, take this book and read it on the way home. If you have any questions, call me. Here's my home telephone number. Even if you just feel like talking, please feel free to call. Evenings are the best time to reach me."

"Thank you so much, Miri. Are they always like that?"

"Yes, Ahuvah. They have to be sure the person is a serious candidate, that his motives for wanting to join the Jewish people are sincere. Don't be afraid of rejection; it's part of the process. To convert to Judaism and to live in Eretz Yisrael, you really have to be determined." Miri continued to reassure me and restore my shattered confidence.

As I was leaving the building, I saw Rabbi Mordechai's friendly face.

"*Shalom*, Ahuvah. I am so sorry to be late, but I went to the wrong place."

"Don't apologize," I said tearfully, realizing at that moment that I had directed him to the wrong office. "I gave you incorrect information."

"How did it go?" he asked.

"Terrible."

"Did you give them my letter?"

"Yes. They totally ignored the letter, and said I should come back when I can speak Hebrew."

"Ahuvah, it's customary," Mordechai said immediately. "They have to turn you away. We don't proselytize. It's forbidden."[2]

"I understand, Mordechai. But did they have to humiliate me?"

"They have to be sure that your motives are pure."

"I am sorry for being so upset, Mordechai. But this was one

---

2 "A convert must initiate his own conversion. It must be volitional. However, once he has applied for conversion, and has proven his sincerity, it is a mitzvah to draw him closer" (ibid., p.19).

of the most humiliating experiences I've ever had."

"Ahuvah, how do you think Ruth felt when Naomi told her to return to her people?"

"Mordechai, I am sure in a day or two I'll see this as an opportunity for spiritual growth. It's encouraging to know that I have two more of these wonderful visits to look forward to! I think I've just discovered a new definition for humility."

I decided to walk to a local restaurant and have a good wholesome meal to cheer myself up. As I walked, I reached down to the deep reservoir of my soul and recited every chapter of *Tehillim* I knew. This spiritual activity revived my *neshamah*.

During lunch, I sat and read the book that Miri had given me, *With All Your Heart* by Rabbi S. Wagschal. I read: "We see that it is possible to achieve victory or success during a moment of intense trust in God, while turning away from Him has the opposite effect." Those words gave me comfort and strengthened me.

Slowly my attention began to shift away from the treatment I had received from the Beis Din and turned again to God. Surely if it were Hashem's will that I leave everything I had and move to Israel, He would bring about the completion of the matter. On many occasions my friends had called me a woman of great faith. I realized after that day's events I would need complete faith for the duration of my journey. My faith had to be elevated to another level. Even though I was disappointed, this was no time to wallow in self-pity. All I knew was that I wanted to convert to Judaism, without any hidden motive. I believed in the God that I had prayed to all those years. I believed in the God of the patriarchs.

Before I went to sleep that night, I prayed: "Dear God, please give me the strength to go through this conversion process properly, and to become one of your chosen people."

I saw the fasten seat belt sign flashing and came back to reality. I was finally home! I couldn't wait for the landing and my taxi ride to Bayit Vegan.

When I saw the familiar sight of Mount Hertzl, my heart started pounding. The leaves on the trees on HaPisgah Street were blowing in the wind. The taxi zoomed. I passed Weisburg Street and the post office, but when I saw the Gra, "my" shul, I knew I was back home.

I spent my first two weeks back home with David and Natanella Ritchie, my dear friends from an earlier visit to Israel. It was like being in heaven. Natanella, a Moroccan, had cooked my favorite dishes for Shabbos: Moroccan fish, Moroccan chicken, and couscous.

The word quickly spread that I was back in Bayit Vegan. My friends were all elated to hear from me. The Beers and the Schwartzbaums were among the first ones I called. In a short time I was booked for Shabbos meals for the next few months; it was comforting to know that I had been so dearly missed.

The school year at Nishmat began two weeks after my arrival. Studying at a seminary for the first time was one of the highlights of my life. Who could imagine such a thing: A forty-nine-year-old Black woman, the granddaughter of sharecroppers, studying at a seminary in Jerusalem. Mind-boggling! Each day I seemed to gain more. "This is the real world," I found myself saying day after day. "This is what I was searching for."

Although I had done numerous exciting things in my life, the experience of learning Torah from such brilliant teachers was unparalleled. I was astonished by the insight of the sages. Even though I had read the books of the Bible for years, I learned now that I had not even scratched the surface. My classmates were accustomed to seeing me teary-eyed. Every time I heard a new idea from Rashi, Ibn Ezra, or the Rambam, my head swam and my heart leaped for joy.

There were times I was able to reciprocate by sharing with the teachers and students knowledge that was unknown to them. My classmates were intrigued by the fact that they had an ex-minister in class. One day in our weekly parashah class, our teacher, Rabbi Baruch Kaplan, explained that the holiday of Thanksgiving in America was taken from the Jewish holiday of Sukkos. I asked Rabbi Kaplan if I could tell the class what my sister's house of worship did during Thanksgiving. They sat spellbound through the entire story.

When I continued, the rabbi commented, "Ahuvah, that's fascinating. I didn't know such a custom existed among Christians!" He thanked me for having taught a lesson on *chesed* in an indirect way.

In my short tenure in Nishmat I became very close to Rebbetzin Chanah Henkin, the founder of the school. The *rebbetzin* had the ability to nurture every girl at the seminary and make her feel at home. She had a motherly approach – one of her hugs could last for months! Since I was looked upon as somewhat of a "matriarch" in the dorm, I received plenty of hugs.

It was time for my second visit to the Beis Din. This time Rabbi Gotthold and Sarah Katz, one of my teachers, accompanied me. The *dayanim* questioned me in Hebrew, but my language skills were still far from what was required; my break from Hebrew lessons during my stay in America was showing. My heart sank when I heard those same closing words. "Come back when you speak Hebrew."

The message was the same, but the tone was different. At least they treated me like a human being this time. I knew now that the judges were not merely parroting a prepackaged spiel delivered to every prospective convert; I knew they meant business.

As Rabbi Gotthold and I were leaving, I asked, "Why are they insisting that I speak Hebrew? I know hundreds of Jews who can't speak it. Is it really necessary?"

"Yes, it is. You must work on your Hebrew, and the next time I think you will pass."

I thanked Rabbi Gotthold and immediately registered at an *ulpan* to learn the language that would make me a Jew.

It became the most unbelievable schedule I'd ever embarked upon. Even when I think about it, I get dizzy! I got up every morning at 6:00 A.M. to daven, shower, and have breakfast before class. My classes at the seminary lasted from 8:30 A.M. to 5:00 P.M., Sunday through Thursday. From 5:00 to 5:30 I traveled by bus to the *ulpan*, where I studied from 5:30 to 8:30 P.M. Afterwards, I'd return to the dorm, have a quick dinner, and go for a walk. From 10:30 to 11:30 P.M., I would study for my conversion until I nearly collapsed. Another shower and off to bed, exhausted. I maintained this marathon schedule five days a week and somehow managed to fit four regular cleaning jobs into my weekly regimen as well.

I was pleased when my young roommates went away for Shabbos. Then I got a wonderful quiet rest that I desperately needed to rejuvenate my tired body and weary mind. Thank God for Shabbos.

On Mondays, we had a half-day session. Afternoons were to be used for doing *chesed*. I had seen this noble quality epitomized by my sister. Every week, I followed her example and ran errands and picked up medicine for an elderly widow. Then I would help my dear friends clean their homes.

On one particular Monday, after I'd finished my *chesed* visits, I had an appointment in town. I asked the owner there if I could use my calling card for a overseas call. I wanted to find out if any of the groups Pnina and I had worked on together had materialized. I had my rabbi's approval to accept commissions from the airlines on tour groups for Christian pilgrimage which I had organized. I was happy to hear that the groups would be coming sporadically.

After a few weeks, I requested another hearing at the Beis Din. When I arrived, I was in for another shock. The clerk told me that my file had been closed. "For what reason?" I asked. But the clerk only spoke Hebrew, so my meeting with him was futile. He sent me to his manager's office, which proved to be pointless as well.

As soon as I left, I anxiously called Rabbi Gotthold to apprise him of the events. I felt that I had come to the end of the road; I didn't think I would ever be accepted.

Rabbi Gotthold did his best to assure me that I shouldn't worry needlessly. "Your motives are pure," he exclaimed. He explained that the Beis Din was highly sensitive to prospective converts who had present or past connections with Christian pastoral activities. A recent bitter experience with another applicant led them to be extra suspicious of conversion being used as a trick by missionaries to covertly make contact with Jewish youth. "Ahuvah, did you tell them you had been a minister?"

"No."

"Then someone else did."

I wondered who would do such a thing.

Rabbi Gotthold and I followed the procedure for reopening the file, only to be told by the clerk that my file could not be found. On our return the next day, we discovered that the file had been locked up in a cabinet in the manager's office. Finally, we were given a date for a new hearing.

Rabbi Gotthold again asked if I had told them that I had been a minister. In his unassuming way, he encouraged me, "Ahuvah, with God's help we will still get everything taken care of." I realized that I couldn't persevere without the help of Rabbi Gotthold. May Hashem bless him for his acts of kindness to a *giyores*!

The date came for our hearing. Rabbi Gotthold had been helping converts for years and he seemed to know everyone in the Beis Din. After the trauma of my first hearing, I felt that, at least, when I walked through the doorway with the rabbi I would be treated with a minimal amount of credibility. But the results of the hearing were not favorable. The Beis Din denied our request to reopen my file.

Frustrated and disappointed, I no longer felt the rabbis in the Beis Din were gorgeous! Rabbi Gotthold explained that the matter was clearly too much responsibility for the lower court to handle. I had to exercise my option and appeal to the Higher Court, the Beis Din HaGadol.

We were informed that the date of the appeal hearing would be given in a few months. I was really being tested on how well I had learned to have faith and trust in God. Before I went to sleep that night I recited some verses from *Yeshayah*: "Youths may weary and tire and young men may constantly falter, but those whose hope is in Hashem will have renewed strength. They will grow wings like eagles; they will run and not grow tired, they will walk and not grow weary" (*Yeshayah* 40:30–31). This was the time that I needed the strength of the eagle that Yeshayah wrote about.

Why, I wondered, had the prophet chosen eagles to make his point? Hoping to acquire a deeper understanding of the passage, I did some research on eagles at the library the next day. I discovered that an eagle doesn't try to avoid bad weather; it flies directly into the storm, and the velocity of the wind bears him above it. When an eagle is wounded, another stands in front of him, flapping its wings until the weaker one's stamina returns. The wounded eagle then stands up and flies again.

I learned a profound lesson from those birds. If an eagle doesn't give up in the face of adversity, neither should I. I would take my "stormy weather" and let it lift me ever higher. Excited by my new discoveries about eagles, I asked Rabbi Kaplan if he could expound more on them.

"In the Torah," he told me, "it says, 'You have seen what I did to Egypt, and that I have borne you on the wings of eagles, and brought you to Me' [*Shemos* 19:4]. Just as the eagle protects its young by absorbing the enemies' arrows into its own body, so the Almighty surrounded our people with the cloud that absorbed the Eygptian arrows."

After hearing this I had complete faith that Hashem would help me overcome the difficulties of my conversion. I knew that He would protect me from the wounds of harsh words.

Over dinner the next day I told my roommates all that had transpired. "Ahuvah," Rivki said, "you'll get through this! Anybody who got through the San Fernando Valley earthquake with such grace can certainly navigate her way through the Jerusalem Beis Din."

"Thank you, Rivki. I really needed to hear that."

Tamara, one of the newest students in the seminary, added, "Ahuvah, your conversion might feel like a spiritual earthquake, but remember — just like Hashem opened the door for you to your apartment, He'll open the door for you to the Beis Din!"

The next day in class we learned about the significance of Hashem's changing the name of my patriarchal "mentor," Avram, to Avraham by adding the Hebrew letter *hei* (*Bereishis* 17:5). It gave him a different and better *mazal*. At lunchtime, I ate quickly. I couldn't wait to go back to my room and meditate on what this new discovery meant to me. Since my name had been changed to Ahuvah, beloved, I hoped that it meant my fate and destiny would also be changed for the better.

One day our class discussed Avraham's leaving his country and family. It was my turn to read and translate when we reached the verse where God promised Avraham that he and his descendants would be a blessing to all the peoples of the world. "And I will make of you a great nation; I will bless you, and make your name great, and you shall be a blessing" (ibid. 12:2).

After I had read and translated the Rashi, I couldn't contain myself; I started crying. When I finished, there were light bulbs going on in my head: *Now, at last, I understand!* Here I was, finally learning the truth contained in Hashem's words. Rashi explained that traveling causes the diminishing of three things: fertility, wealth, and one's fame and reputation. I thought of how far I had traveled in my life, both geographically and culturally. I told the rest of the class I thought I knew how Avraham felt: "It must be something like what I am feeling."

I reflected once more on the haunting verse: "Go for yourself from your land, from your relatives, and from your father's house...." As Rashi adds — "for yourself" indicates "for your own benefit." In order to join the Jewish people, I had to separate myself emotionally from my family. This was not something that could happen overnight; the process took place over an extended period of time. I began to appreciate Hashem's mercy in extending my spiritual journey until I was ready for what had to be done.

It was Shabbos, but the normal tranquility of the day was constantly broken by the phone's shrill ring; we'd forgotten to unplug it before Shabbos began. My roommate Judy wondered if it was bad news from someone's family in the States. Her intuition was uncannily accurate.

After Havdalah, I answered the telephone. "Hello, Lobo. I've been trying to reach you. The hospital called and said Daddy stopped breathing."

"What does that mean?" I refused to comprehend what she'd just told me.

"It means he's not breathing." I was dumbfounded. *Hashem, please, it's my Daddy, my last parent.* "Nellie, could you please verify that and call me back?"

Five minutes later, my sister called back and told me that my father had died in his sleep. I hung up the telephone and went for a walk. I wasn't in contact with my feelings; I was numb. As I paced my usual route, I recited my Daddy's favorite *Tehillim*, Psalm 24, and my mother's favorite, Psalm 27. Then I breathed in the inevitable truth of verse 10: "Though my father and mother have forsaken me, Hashem will gather me in."

After all the years I had walked around reciting that verse, only in that lonely moment of truth, dolefully walking through the streets of Jerusalem, could I fully understand and appreciate it from the depths of my heart: "Mother and Daddy, I hope you're getting along up there. It's You and me now, God!"

As I approached the stairs leading to the dorm, these words came to my lips: "Had I not trusted that I would see the goodness of Hashem in the Land of the Living!" (*Tehillim* 27:13). That verse was prophetic for me; my entire support group from the seminary was there with hugs and kisses and tears, asking if there was anything they could do.

"You've done enough! Just being here is enough," was all I could say to them. Oh, how I wished I could have cried with them. I was still in shock.

The next morning, I went to class with special vigor. My father had always admired my studying; what better way to honor him? Praying and studying Torah was the only way I could stand on my feet. Rebbetzin Henkin spoke to me at lunchtime. She gave me a big hug and said, "Ahuvah, is there anything we can do?" If there was, she certainly did it with her hug and loving concern.

"When are you leaving?" she asked sympathetically.

"I don't know, because I don't want to go."

The *rebbetzin* looked at me and said, "Ahuvah, make every effort to go." One more hug for reassurance and I was ready to board the plane. As I walked to class, I managed to let out a few tears.

Leah, one of my seminary friends, arranged a *seudah* in memory of my father the next day. All the girls from both the Hebrew and English programs were present. They baked lasagna, kugel, and a variety of Israeli salads, and bought me a gorgeous bouquet of flowers. Those girls, all my juniors, were always there when I needed them.

After we ate, they asked me to tell them about my father. Hesitantly at first, I began to speak.

"My parents divorced when I was a small child. After my father had retired from driving a taxi, he took up farming, like his parents before him. He bought twenty-five acres of land in St. Anne, Illinois, and built a home there. Every year he would bring us crowder peas. How I loved those crowder peas!

"My father was a man with a great sense of humor. But there is more to life than making people laugh. I don't ever remember my father holding me as a child. My sister Nellie always used to say that our father was a sensitive person, carrying around a burden of shame for his past mistakes. As the years went by I began to feel that perhaps she was right. For many years, I prayed to close the huge gap between my father and myself. I wanted so desperately to love and respect him. It was not until I was already well into my adult life that we were able to develop some closeness.

"I was forty-two years old when my father came to Beverly Hills to visit Nellie and me. On that visit I told my father how he had hurt me as a child because he was emotionally unavailable. I had to tell him in love; it was a heart-rinsing experience! I curled up in his arms and cried like a baby. From that time on, we were the best of friends."

Even in my pain I could smile at a memory of my father, who was hardly a seasoned traveler.

"One summer Nellie and I took a special trip to our grandparents. Nellie flew in from California, and Daddy and I left from Illinois, he from St. Anne and I from Chicago. We all met in Jackson, Mississippi. It was one of those unforgettable family trips.

"We were flying on Delta to Lexington, Mississippi. After we went through the airline security, I told Daddy that I would go ahead to the gate to put our names on the stand-by list.

"When Daddy came to the gate I noticed he didn't have his luggage. 'Where's your luggage?' I asked.

" 'Doesn't the skycap bring it down to the gate?'

" 'No, he doesn't. Where did you leave it?'

" 'On the conveyor belt.'

" 'Okay, please sit down over there and don't move. I'll be right back.'

"I hurried back to the conveyor belt and asked the security agent if she had seen a small black bag. Sure enough, it was on the conveyor belt exactly where he had left it." My friends chuckled. I continued with my narrative, again growing teary-eyed.

"The last time I saw my father was just one year ago, when he picked me up at O'Hare Airport to visit my brother, Ezra, after his operation. During the drive to Ezra's, I thanked God — finally I could laugh at my father's jokes. We cried when we painfully reminisced about the love of our lives – Mother!

"The fifth commandment says: 'Honor your father and your mother, so that your days will be lengthened upon the land that Hashem, your God, gives you.' I was not obligated to keep this commandment the way that a Jew by birth is, but I was raised on this precept. In my heart, though, I had not fulfilled it until that momentous day in Beverly Hills."

When I finished they were all in tears. I was grateful that Hashem had given me the right words to honor my father's memory.

Then Judy broke the silence and called out in her New York accent: "Come on, Ahuvah, quote us some *tehillim*!"

Leah added, "You go, girl!"

In marked contrast to the somber way we had started, we ended up in laughter.

Nellie flew to Chicago and made all the arrangements for the interment. I was indebted to my family that they held up the proceedings until I could collect myself emotionally and make my final decision. It was extremely difficult for me to go to America; I didn't want to see my last parent dead. I went to Rabbi Heyman and explained my situation. His reply was, "Ahuvah, Avraham Avinu went to his father's funeral out of honor to his father." I was aboard the next plane.

When I finally arrived in Chicago, my sister, brothers, and I went to pay respects to our daddy. (Although Ezra Jr. was not Daddy's son but the son of my step-father, Ezra Sr., he shared our sorrow and we mourned as a family.) I'll remember that painful day forever. My sister sobbed uncontrollably. If I could have taken some of her pain, I would have gladly done so! I was asked by my family to eulogize my father. I declined; I felt I didn't have the strength. In his honor I read his favorite *Tehillim*, Psalm 24. Following the funeral all I could do was get on the plane and return immediately to Israel.

I find it ironic that I would be writing this part of my book during the month of March, just a few days before my Daddy's birthday. In a sense, I feel as if he and my mother are here with me. All the tears that I was unable to shed at his funeral, I've managed to release here in the quiet confines of my beautiful apartment in Bayit Vegan. It's as if I had to relive the agony of losing them over and over again. I pray that by sharing all my painful experiences I will be able to bring solace to everyone who reads this book, as I myself found comfort.

When I arrived back at the seminary, the *rebbetzin* was the

first to greet me. She threw her arms around me. I thanked her for
encouraging me to go.

Every morning, hearing the sounds of prayer from the
Sephardic shul nearby gave me strength to get out of bed. Day by
day, my strength increased while I prayed and studied Torah. A
week after my return, I received a letter from the higher court in
the Old City of Jerusalem, informing me of the date when I was to
appear. I took the letter to the *rebbetzin*. She called a meeting with
her associate, Rebbetzin Riva Sperling, and my *chavrusa*, Chani
Diamont. Together, they devised a plan. One hour of my study-
time in the morning would be dedicated to Hebrew, and one
hour in the afternoon for study toward the conversion. Riva was
going to go with me to the higher court.

Although I was twice Chani's age, we were very close. She
was an excellent teacher and made me work hard. She never ut-
tered empty words of sympathy; instead she motivated me to try
harder. "You know this word. We just had it yesterday." I knew
the words. It was just a matter of trying to get my brain to function. I had been so traumatized; I just wanted all this pressure to
be over. I wanted a normal life.

Chani and I worked extremely hard reviewing the laws of
kashrus. I also memorized the Jewish calendar with the Jewish
festivals and their dates and meaning. To make sure that I was
prepared, Chani had me memorize the thirty-nine *avos
melachah* in Hebrew.

Rabbi Dovid Sperling, Riva's husband, taught us the laws of
Shabbos from *Shemirath Shabbath*. Once I went to them for
Shabbos and their little son Ettiel helped me with my Hebrew. He
was a natural teacher, just like his dad. He kept asking me, "Do
you understand, Ahuvah?" I nodded politely.

A week before my fourth hearing, a friend saw that I was looking very somber during dinner. "Ahuvah," she asked, "is everything okay? You look so sad."

"I think the seriousness of my decision is weighing on me," I told her. "There are six hundred and thirteen mitzvos for a Jew to keep. Right now, I only have to keep seven. I just have to trust that the same God who brought me this far will help me fulfill the remaining six hundred and six."

The date finally arrived for the hearing. Rabbi Gotthold, with some understanding of human nature (as well as of the judicial process), told me, "The hearing is preliminary, and not the test. It is just to see if they will reopen the file."

"That is fine with me. Besides, they have already turned me down three times! What's one more time?"

Osnat Goldman, Natanella's neighbor, lent me a beautiful skirt, blouse, and sweater to wear. I wore my hair in a ponytail, and I had on a pearl necklace and earrings. Simi Peters, a teacher at Nishmat, had me try on the outfit to make sure it was appropriate. The girls in the dorm said that I looked *chareidi*. Leah said, "Ahuvah, you were born *chareidi*."

The director of my seminary, Rabbi Zvi Blobstein, verified with the higher court that the Sephardi chief rabbi, known historically as the *rishon leTzion*, Rabbi Eliyahu Bakshi-Doron, would conduct the interview. No one had ever heard of such a thing! The chief rabbi normally doesn't get involved in conversions. I just wanted it over, and so did the rest of the neighborhood. As Riva and I traveled to the Old City, I remembered what Sheefra had said; I was beginning to wonder if I would make it through alive.

Rabbi Bakshi-Doron interviewed me intensively for about

twenty minutes. He was such a gentleman and followed careful protocol. In the beginning, we spoke in Hebrew. When we got to the more difficult questions, Riva asked if she could translate for me. So I spoke to Riva in English and she spoke to the rabbi in Hebrew. Rabbi Gotthold sat quietly.

Then Rabbi Bakshi-Doron looked at me and in perfect English asked me if I would leave the room, because he needed to speak with Rabbi Gotthold. When I left the room, I recited every chapter of *tehillim* I knew. In approximately ten minutes they called me back in and I was tested extensively. Rabbi Bakshi-Doron conducted the entire interview. He asked me how to *kasher* chicken. I was so glad I had read that in a book a few years before. We spent a lot of time on questions relating to tea essence for Shabbos. He asked me about the holiday of Sukkos specifically. Everything he asked, I knew.

In half an hour we were finished. At the end of my session, the rabbi thanked me and told me I would be hearing from them in a few days. I didn't know whether I had passed or not.

When we left, Rabbi Gotthold and Riva said simultaneously, "Ahuvah, that was great! You must have passed." I wasn't as confident as they were. In my mind I assumed I would have to go back at least one more time.

Some weeks later, Riva told me a little more of what had gone on in these deliberations. "When you left the room, do you know what Rabbi Bakshi-Doron asked Rabbi Gotthold? He looked at him and said, 'Gotthold, when you get to *Shamayim* are you willing to testify that this woman is committed to *Yiddishkeit*?' Rabbi Gotthold answered, 'Yes.' "

There were a few weeks left to Pesach; I had been cleaning houses until I was ready to drop. I called one of the rabbis in the

Beis Din every day for eight days to determine if I had passed the test. Then, finally, he opened the door to my future.

Wearied by all my telephone calls, he said, "Ahuvah, you're a *Yehudiah*. We're just waiting for the third signature. You can come and pick up the papers tomorrow."

The next morning I went to pick up my conversion papers from the Beis Din HaGadol. They told me that I had to pick up a slip from my conversion file to take with me to the *mikveh*. I decided to ask Natanella to go with me the next morning, even though there were only three weeks left before Pesach.

When Natanella and I arrived at the office to get the approval I needed for the *mikveh*, I was in for yet another shock. Natanella understood the Hebrew conversation. She told me, "Ahuvah, they're talking about you."

"What are they saying?"

"They are saying, 'She's the one who was the minister, that missionary!' Ahuvah, they even checked you out in the States. There was someone who didn't want you to convert."

I was stunned. "Now I understand why I had such difficulty. Someone has given them erroneous information."

"No one wants to have anything to do with your file. It's a hot potato!"

"Tell them we're not leaving until we get that approval letter. I have to have it for the *mikveh* tomorrow morning."

Finally, after much persistence on Natanella's part, they found my file and gave me the authorization. When you are facing a crisis, Natanella is a good person to know. I left the office that day firmly clutching the ticket to my new life.

On my way home, I stopped by a family that I was very close to. I shared the events of the entire day with them. When they heard what I'd been through, they relayed the following story:

Apparently, someone who had overheard my phone conversation with Pnina about the Christian tour groups, a call I'd made on a pay phone months before, had misconstrued it entirely. That person called the Beis Din and told them I was an ordained minister and a Christian missionary. Finally, I knew the reason why my file had been closed!

The informer gave the Beis Din the name of two families in Bayit Vegan who knew me well. Yad L'Achim, an anti-missionary organization, contacted the families, who rallied to my support. The first family they called told them that the information was erroneous and that only a very vicious person would do such a thing. The second family actually went down to the office of Yad L'Achim to meet with the director. The director ran my name through a computer bank; the results made it clear that the information was false.

Neither of the families had wanted to tell me anything about the incident. They felt (not without good reason) that emotionally I had been through enough, with the recent loss of my father. Now, in an obvious turn of *hashgachah peratis*, I had dropped by one of these families!

As I thought of all the torment this anonymous informer had caused me, I felt I had to draw upon all the ethical lessons I'd learned in seminary. "We have to give the person the benefit of the doubt, even though it caused me unimaginable pain and difficulty," I finally said. "In his mind he probably felt he was doing the right thing. I have to judge him favorably." My prayer is that this story will serve as a vital message to all of us about the devastating effects of *lashon hara*.

My conversion process had taken two years. When it was

over I realized how much fine-tuning had taken place in my life. Only Hashem knows when the time is right.

Natanella offered to accompany me to the *mikveh*. While we were waiting for the *mikveh* superintendent to arrive, the two of us took a walk, admiring the glorious spring blossoms. I felt I had reached the culmination of my journey of faith. It was just three weeks before Pesach, almost the beginning of Nissan. Nissan is the month of the liberation of the Jewish people from the Egyptian bondage, the month of new beginnings...and a month which was packed with so many precious memories for the prelude to my conversion.

I dipped three times in the *mikveh*, and after arising from the waters exclaimed, "Natanella, I'm a Jew."

True to the sacred Jewish tradition that a convert receives a new *neshamah*, I can testify that when I came out of that water — crowned with a Jewish soul — I was a different person. On the twenty-fourth of the Jewish month Adar, in the year 5757 from the Creation of the World (April 2, 1997), I entered the fresh purifying waters of the *mikveh*. One life-journey had drawn to a close, and my new journey of faith had only just begun.

My conversion had been the talk of the Ritchies' home for the past few days. When Natanella and I arrived at their door on our return from the *mikveh*, Avraham Moshe exclaimed in Hebrew, "But Ahuvah, how come you're still black?" I laughed; even this little child knew the essence of my going to the *mikveh*.

My sister called later that day to wish me a happy birthday. "Fifty-one years ago, Christine had a little baby girl. Happy birthday, Lobo."

"Nellie, you won't believe it, but I went to the *mikveh* today."

"Yeah!" she cheered. "We did it!"

A few days later, I received the most memorable birthday gift in my life: a lovely card — with one hundred dollars — that said, "Congratulations, my sister the Jew. We're proud of you. Love, Nellie and Ezra."

Instinctively, I knew the title for the book I had wanted to write my entire life: *My Sister, the Jew.*

What a birthday present! I thought. Reborn at fifty-one! "The Talmud writes, '*Ger shenisgayeir kekatan shenolad damei* — One who has become a proselyte is like a child newly born' (*Yevamos* 22a), to describe the convert's rebirth. As a new person, he has no connection with his past, and as a result of his conversion attains atonement for all his sins."[3]

When I was a little girl, I used to pray that God would change my birthday. It seemed like it always rained on April 2. Bad weather prevented my childhood friends from coming to my party, so my birthday memories are mostly sad. I was thrilled that Hashem had answered my childhood prayers.

Rebbetzin Henkin had requested emphatically that I come directly back to Nishmat after my immersion. When we arrived, however, we found the office locked. *That's strange,* I thought. Then I remembered that the *rebbetzin* had said to come directly to the *beis midrash.* In the large room we were greeted with multi-colored balloons and a bright pink and green sign which read, "*Mazal tov,* Ahuvah."

What a fantastic way to start a new life! I touched the mezuzah, kissed my fingers, took a deep breath, and walked through the door of the *beis midrash,* for the first time as a Jew.

---

3 (Schwartz, Rabbi Yoel. Jewish Conversion, p. 26.)

The entire seminary was there, as were many of my friends from the neighborhood. They were singing, "*Siman tov u'mazal tov.*" I didn't know whether to laugh or cry. Before I knew it, I was pulled into a circle to dance.

When we raised our wine glasses to make the traditional "*l'chaim,*" I waited for the *rebbetzin* or one of our teachers to make the *berachah* on my behalf. But by popular request, I made the *berachos* for the entire group. I felt a joy that I had never felt before — a joy rooted in holiness and purity. Until that moment, people had always made the appropriate blessings for me. It was the first time in my life that I could do so for others. I felt particularly honored because the *rebbetzin* never canceled classes for anything. This cancellation of classes had to come straight from the top, from Hashem.

Rebbetzin Henkin gave the most beautiful, touching *shiur* on *Megillas Rus* I've ever heard in my life. Then she took me by the hand up to the podium, adjusted the microphone, and said, "Ahuvah, this is a special day for us. We are very grateful that we were able to be a part of your conversion process. Can you share with us in your own words how you're feeling at this moment?"

All my little sisters shouted, "Speech, speech!"

I was so overcome by their love that the only thing I could think to say was, "I am speechless!" Then I cleared my throat and tried to regain my composure. "I have traveled all over the world. I've conducted seminars and given hundreds of lectures, and I've had many incredible experiences. But my decision to join the Jewish people was the most important decision I have ever made in my life.

"There are some people who aren't here today because they have entered the next world. I feel I would very much like to thank and acknowledge them. No other family of a prospective convert could possibly offer her the kind of support which I received from my family.

"Just before I moved to Israel my mother died, and, recently, my father died and my brother suffered a massive heart attack. Through all those experiences, you, my dear friends, gave me your love and support. It gives me such *chizuk* to be connected to the Jewish people. You have taken me in and cared for me. You've all shown me such depth of feeling. I don't know if I've ever experienced this kind of love and support in my entire life. The kindness that you have shown me is something that I will always treasure." There wasn't a dry eye in the *beis midrash*.

On that day my childhood fantasy of wanting to be like Princess Grace of Monaco had come true. I had become a Jewish princess.

Chapter 10

When I've Come to the End of the Road

"**B**lessed are You, Hashem, Who separates between holy and secular." My hosts for *seudah shelishis* had concluded the Shabbos with Havdalah. *What a beautiful time of rest the seventh day is*, I thought. As I walked home, the aroma of spices, cinnamon, and cloves lingered, strengthening my soul for the new week.

Once I arrived home, I checked my messages. "Hello, Delores! This is Sheila Cohen (not her actual name). I hope you remember me. We'd like to come to Israel soon, and we'd love to see you. Sorry you're not in right now. I know it's the Sabbath there, but we'll try again tomorrow."

Sheila Cohen! A voice from the past. How did she know my telephone number? When was the last time I saw her family? It must have been four or five years before. How wonderful to have someone I knew coming to Israel! What was her husband's name? I couldn't remember. They had a lovely little girl. *If only they'd left their number, I could call back*, I thought.

That night, I thought about the call again. What did Sheila

mean, they'd like to come to Israel? Did she mean for a visit, to tour the country for a few weeks? Many Christians come here on a pilgrimage to visit the Christian sites. *Oh, no! What if they invite me to come along? I'll just have to explain that the halachah prevents me from doing so.*

Actually, Sheila and I had been only acquaintances in the States. She must have gone to great lengths to track me down. I wondered why. Memories flooded my mind as I lingered between sleep and consciousness. They had joined my place of worship and become very active there. I began to remember more. Her husband had been born and raised Jewish, in an Orthodox home. His father had died young, and as a result of that painful experience the son had left Judaism and become a born-again Christian. Sheila was an African-American. I recalled that they used to drive a long distance to services on Sunday. It must have taken them about an hour and a half each way! Eager to reconnect with someone from my past, I still couldn't help wondering. Could it be possible that they had become interested in Judaism? After exhausting all possibilities, I fell asleep imagining the Cohens experiencing a Shabbos in Bayit Vegan.

Because I've been accustomed to a two-day weekend my entire life, Sunday is my slowest day. I find it extremely difficult to make the transformation from the spiritual bliss of Shabbos to the mundane. Sluggishly I trudged through my usual routine – *Modeh Ani*, washing hands, showering, dressing, praying, and eating hot oatmeal for breakfast. Before running to catch the bus to Har Nof, I checked my telephone. I heard, "Hi, Delores! It's Sheila Cohen again. I guess it's too early over there to phone you now. You must still be sleeping. We'll try again later."

I had started attending Neve Yerushalayim seminary immediately after Pesach, 1997. During Chumash class there the next day, I stared at the Hebrew letters, not really seeing them. It was not until two nights later, after two more missed phone calls, that I finally spoke to Sheila in person. "Hello, Delores? This is Sheila Cohen. I don't know if you remember me, but...."

"Of course, I remember you," I interrupted. "I am thrilled that you're planning to visit Israel."

She laughed, "Oh, no! Not a visit! We're planning to make aliyah."

"What!" Despite all my speculations, I was completely unprepared for Sheila's announcement.

More surprises were in store. We spoke for about forty-five minutes, during which Sheila asked not only about aliyah, but also about converting to Judaism. "Is aliyah easier to make from the States?" she asked.

"Yes. There's a lot of bureaucracy here and it will be much simpler for you to just go through the Jewish Agency office in Los Angeles."

"We did check with them. They advised us to make a pilot trip, since we have never been to Israel before."

"Well, that's good advice. But what is it that makes you think of converting to Judaism?"

"Oh, we're just so thoroughly disappointed in all the services we've attended. We really prefer the synagogue."

"Well, you know, I converted to Judaism."

"And are you happy?"

"Oh, yes! Happier than I've ever been in my life!"

I assured Sheila that I'd be more than delighted to help her family in any way I could, and we agreed to stay in touch. I had just one more question.

"By the way, how did you ever find me?"

"The Lord told me to call you. It took months, but I finally tracked you down through your ex-husband Henry."

Immediately, I called Yosef and told him the story.

"Yosef," I said earnestly, "I feel that Hashem has placed me in Eretz Yisrael to help others whose journey will follow mine."

Yosef had many questions, and I sensed his hesitation at raising some of them. "You know, Ahuvah, the halachah is that a *kohein* can't marry a convert. I would guess from their last name that her husband is a *kohein*, which is very problematic. Did you mention that to Sheila?"

"No, I did think of that, but if he's done *teshuvah* I didn't want to disillusion them."

I could hear Yosef inhale audibly. "This could be a major problem. Try to find out if they're studying somewhere, and ask them if they have a rabbi," he suggested.

At Yosef's urging, I phoned Sheila. "Do you and Simon have a rabbi that you're studying with?"

"Oh, no, we don't have anyone like that. The only synagogue out here is Reform, and the rabbi doesn't seem to know very much. But we do enjoy going to synagogue very much."

"Was it your idea to start going to the temple?"

"Yes, it was, Delores." We laughed. "Was it very hard for you, Delores, leaving your old friends, family, and all, to become a Jew?"

"Yes, most people don't understand. I'm sure they're still praying for my salvation. Well...let them!" We laughed again.

"The fact that we're an interracial couple hasn't been easy for either of our families. And we haven't told them about this pending move."

How I empathized with her. "Sheila, Jerusalem is waiting for you and your family. We will be your family. I've already started apartment hunting for you. I've had such love and support from the people of my neighborhood and I'm sure you will, too. Some have already told me they would like to meet you and your family." We hung up on that positive note, and I was growing increasingly excited for the Cohens' future.

I called Yosef with the Cohens' address so he could mail them some material from his Web site, Chazon, a course for Jews seeking their heritage.

Again, I sensed he was being cautious. "Ahuvah, I've spoken to someone with more expertise in these matters. Maybe you should advise Sheila to rethink her plans. If they came here, their kids would have to go to nonreligious schools. The religious schools couldn't accept them until they'd become Jewish. Not being accepted into the local community might be very traumatic for them. We also need to find a rabbi for the Cohens to consult with — someone in California."

Rabbi Brown (not his actual name) was recommended to me for the Cohens. I had actually spoken to him before I made aliyah, and I knew they would be in good hands with him. When I phoned her again, Sheila seemed unconcerned about the children's schooling; she explained that she was home-schooling them, anyhow. They were still very determined to go ahead, no matter what the obstacles.

"Sheila," I said, "I've been thinking that Old Katamon might be a better neighborhood for you. It's more diversified, with lots of young families and singles, and a very relaxed atmosphere. It also has some very nice synagogues."

"Are there any Conservative ones?"

"No, but all different kinds of Orthodox."

I was very concerned about the halachah that a *kohein* is forbidden to marry a convert, but I still felt it was too soon to press this matter, in spite of Yosef's persistence. I could only hope they would follow the suggestion of seeking out a rabbi, whereupon the subject would inevitably be addressed and in a more appropriate form.

Meanwhile, Pesach was just three weeks away, and I had to complete cleaning my own home, as well as the homes of scores of customers for my cleaning service. I was tempted to let the matter rest until after Pesach.

In my parashah class at Neve, I learned about how Moshe assumed the office of the *kohein* for seven days until he installed Aharon and his sons (*Shemos*, ch. 40). As I studied the seriousness of being a *kohein*, the issue began to weigh heavily on my mind. Sheila had to be told as soon as possible, I decided. My mind was buzzing with questions. Maybe Simon was not really a *kohein*? Or perhaps there was some disqualifying factor in his background that would permit him to marry a convert?

It was two days before Pesach when I phoned Sheila again. I couldn't go into Pesach with all this ambiguity. "I have been thinking about you," I told her. "Have you been in touch with Rabbi Brown yet?"

"I was planning to phone him after Passover."

"I see. Tell me, did anyone ever mention to you that a *kohein* isn't allowed to marry a convert?"

"Oh, yeah. But it's too late now! He's not going to divorce me!"

I knew that my moment of truth had arrived. "Sheila, the laws of the Torah are very explicit. They are eternal laws from

Mount Sinai. They've never changed, and they won't ever change. That's one of the things that attracted me to Judaism — its authenticity."

Calmly and with great empathy I continued, "Just as you are busy packing all your boxes and putting them in order, so too must you speak with a rabbi before you leave Los Angeles, and set your spiritual house in order."

There was no response. Very softly, I said, "Sheila, we live very disciplined lives." A verse from *Tehillim* came to my mind, and I shared it with her: "I will educate you and enlighten you in which path to go; I will advise you with what my eye has seen" (32:8).

Before I hung up, I stressed the importance of consulting Simon's mother to ascertain if he was in fact a *kohein*. Perhaps he had something that would disqualify him from the priesthood. I also urged her to check out her own family background; perhaps she had some Jewish maternal ancestors. Knowing that I had done all I could, I was relieved and able to enjoy Pesach with my mind undisturbed.

Classes at Neve resumed the Sunday after Pesach. I was happy to see everyone after the four-week break. The corridors and classrooms were buzzing with excitement. Although it was delightful to settle back into the classroom routine, my mind kept wandering back to the Cohen family.

That evening, I felt compelled to phone.

"Oh, Delores!" Sheila said upon hearing my voice. "Simon's mother says he's a real *kohein*, and not disqualified."

"I see.... Have you spoken to Rabbi Brown?"

"Not yet."

I was beginning to develop some grave concerns and was

even becoming a bit annoyed by her lack of follow up. Once again I reminded Sheila of the urgent need to meet with a rabbi before coming on aliyah, wondering when and if my efforts would be fruitful.

Sheila ended our conversation on an optimistic note: "Delores, whatever happens, I just want you to know that I'm glad you gave me all the facts. No matter what the situation is, I really prefer to know."

Wearied, I began to lose sleep thinking about the Cohen family. Their potential tragedy was causing great pain, for them and for me.

The sequence of events was uncanny. Sheila had tracked me down, to Bayit Vegan, Jerusalem, after not having been in touch with me for four years. Her desire to convert was filled with problematic halachos pertaining to *kohanim*. The parashiyos read after Pesach continued to discuss the laws of the priesthood. Though I'd covered the whole book of Leviticus (*Vayikra*) every year for the last eighteen years, I was beginning to realize that I had never fully understood the significance of the priesthood of Aharon. Perhaps this loaded spiritual bombshell that had fallen into my lap was *bashert*, forcing me, as I studied the Hebrew text, to slowly absorb the truth.

Soon after Pesach, during the parashah of *Acharei Mos–Kedoshim*, an article appeared in the Ohrnet Shabbos Torah handout regarding the *kehunah*. It tugged at my heartstrings. A most moving scene was described in the Mishnah (text paraphrased):

> *When the kohein gadol went to perform the Yom Kippur service, a bitter dispute raged between the Elders of the Sanhedrin and the Sadducees about the means whereby the kohein gadol would offer the incense. So serious was the issue that the elders of the*

Sanhedrin made the kohein gadol swear that he would not change anything of all which they required of him.

Then, in a dramatic moment before the awesome Yom Kippur service, both the kohein gadol and the elders turned aside from each other and wept. The elders wept because they suspected the high priest of being a Sadducee. The kohein gadol wept because they had reason to be suspicious of him.

I too wept now, staring in the face of the humbling and inescapable truth: no other priesthood could ever replace the priesthood of Aharon. Any tampering with the priesthood is no longer Judaism. I wept because here was this good Christian woman trying against such daunting forces to lead her husband, a *kohein*, back to his *Yiddishkeit*.

I called Sheila again to tell her of my conversation with a rabbi who promised to work with the Cohen family, but solely with the understanding that Simon was returning to Judaism. I told the rabbi that Sheila was a Christian, but we didn't discuss the halachic issues of the situation.

During my previous conversation with Sheila, she had expressed a deep concern regarding the integration of her children into a religious neighborhood. I acknowledged her concern, explaining to her that in the *chareidi* world religious children and non-religious children do not usually intermingle; I had selected Old Katamon for them because it was a community with more diversity.

The next time I called, Sheila wasn't home. Her daughter answered and handed the phone to her father. I enthusiastically informed Simon of the new developments. "I found an Orthodox rabbi in a pluralistic neighborhood who is willing to accept your family."

"Well, that's fine, but I am messianic," Simon said almost with a snarl.

"I see," I said, barely able to squeeze out the words. "Please inform your wife that I called."

I hung up, stunned. The hostility in Simon's voice was palpable. It was apparent that Simon was not in the least bit interested in reconnecting with his Jewish roots. His interest was to move to Israel as a messianic missionary.

I suffered another night with sleep eluding me. The next morning after praying, I couldn't wait to share the whole story with Yosef. Both of us agreed that it had been Hashem's way of allowing me to find out the truth about the Cohens — before I caused a lot of embarrassment to many well-meaning families and myself.

I decided to call Sheila back and tell her I was unable to help her. I thought I had made it very clear to her that I had joined the Jewish people and I no longer practiced the non-Jewish teachings. Sheila had indicated to me that she wanted to convert and was interested in becoming Jewish. What a deceitful person!

This time Sheila answered the phone; she sounded cheerful. I felt the conversation was being recorded in the heavenly archives. I knew I had to be true to my heart's convictions. "Did your husband tell you we had spoken?"

"Yes."

"When I spoke to your husband, he informed me that he was a messianic Jew. Messianic Judaism is antithetical to Judaism; we are forbidden to make any human being into a god. Your husband is a Jew. Therefore, in all good conscience, there is no way I can take you to an Orthodox rabbi unless your husband is willing to become a true observant Jew."

It wasn't easy, but I continued to speak, my voice trembling just a little, "Perhaps you won't thank me now, but further on down the road you'll realize that I am giving you the best possible advice I know. You and your children would be better off staying in America. Think about your children. You can't put them into a religious school, and they will not be able to marry Jews. In addition to that, there's the language barrier.

"Even Jewish families that have moved here sometimes return to their country of origin, unable to make the required adjustments in Israel.

"I hope you understand my position. When I went before the Jerusalem Beis Din, I took an oath that the Jewish people are my people and their God is my God. As a Jewess, only by maintaining and striving to strengthen my own unique heritage can I possess something special to give to all humanity. If you and your family are still committed to Christian or messianic beliefs, there are many organizations who will cater to your needs.

"Sheila, in a few days Jews will be celebrating Shavuos. On Sunday morning before sunrise, Jews from every corner of Jerusalem will be walking to the Western Wall to pray the morning service. When that morning arrives, I will stand before the Almighty. I have to do so with a clear conscience and a pure heart. I wish you and your family much success and happiness, but I can't help you. I have to be true to the Jewish people who are now my family."

After I finished, a few moments of pensive silence ensued. In the end, Sheila responded, "I understand, Delores. When you go to the Western Wall on Shavuos morning, will you pray for my family?"

I was so furious with Sheila and her facade that my hands

were shaking when I hung up the phone. She had been lying to me the entire time, in order to carry out her scheme. The results of such an incident would have been devastating.

I sat quietly in my chair facing *mizrach*. I thought about the question that the Chief Rabbi had asked Rabbi Gotthold. I thought about the informer that had given the Beis Din erroneous information. I also thought about the families and my seminaries that had been so loving and accepting of me. I felt that in this incident I had passed a crucial test. I had come to the end of the road.

My prayers were very special that morning. When I came to the Shema, the Jew's solemn declaration of the unity of the Creator of Heaven and Earth, I whispered with great emotion, "*Baruch sheim kevod malchuso leolom va'ed* – Blessed is the Name of His glorious kingdom for all eternity."

Getting to Know You

A fter my conversion I would occasionally visit close friends for Shabbos. One Friday afternoon, as I approached the front steps of the Goldbergs' home in Old Katamon, I heard a soul-stirring *niggun* of Shlomo Carlebach coming through the doorway. I walked into the kitchen and found the family humming along with the tape that was playing. It seemed as if the entire family was busy with his or her assigned duties for bringing in and welcoming the Shabbos. In such an aura of happiness, I felt compelled to join in, too.

Avigail made the chicken soup and zucchini quiche while I fried the chicken, Southern style, and made the peach cobbler. (I had long ago learned to use margarine instead of butter, so my old favorite peach cobbler would be pareve.) While I was chopping up the salads, I felt more at home than I had for a long time. Preparing my favorite recipes for my friends was my way of reciprocating the warmth and friendship they had shown me when I first came to Israel.

When we sat down for Kiddush on Shabbos evening, I thought about a verse from *Koheles*: "Everything has its season, and there is a time for everything under the heaven" (3:1). The time I spend with the Goldbergs will always bring back fond memories; they anchored me in the Jewish way of life. Those informal Shabbos meals and the preciously sweet and friendly children warmed and nurtured my heart and soul. But as much as I loved that family, I still missed my own neighborhood too much to remain in Old Katamon long.

In June 1997 I left the Nishmat dormitory and moved in with a lovely couple, Shmuel and Channah Katz (not their real names), on Rechov Bayit Vegan. I had the special privilege of living with the Katzes for two months. My bedroom was opposite the room of their six-month-old baby boy. Every morning when I said *Modeh Ani* and washed my hands, I used to see him peering out of the bars of his crib and laughing.

During my stay under the roof of this unique couple, I learned more Torah than I could ever have while sitting in a classroom. What I saw in their lives was Torah in action. I will always cherish the memories of that time when I was given an opportunity to live with a couple who'd been brought up in observant homes from birth.

One day Channah said, "Ahuvah, let's go over your food cabinet and see what you have." The results of the inventory of my tiny pantry were startling: we had a pile of things which could be used and a pile of things which could not be used. I had always assumed that everything I bought in Yerushalayim was kosher. "Channah, you mean I've been cooking food with the wrong *hechsher* in a kosher kitchen?"

With her usual calm demeanor she replied, "Do you know that when Shmuel first moved to Israel he did exactly the same thing? Until he checked it out, he thought that everything sold in Israel was *glatt kosher!*"

One hot summer's day, Channah asked me, "Aren't you boiling?"

"Not really. I guess it's my African blood," I joked.

She said, "I'm more African than you are."

I was puzzled for a moment. But then I remembered that my friend had been born in South Africa. "You're absolutely right, you are more African than I."

That conversation brought home to me the wonderful realization that people from diverse backgrounds within Judaism can come together and live in harmony with one another without ever feeling any hostility or prejudice.

One night at the dinner table we were discussing one of the books of Rabbi Matityahu Glazerson. Channah said to me, "Ahuvah, you can meet the author this Shabbos; the Glazersons are coming over for dinner."

I sat stunned; I had no idea that one of my favorite authors lived in Bayit Vegan. *How wonderful to have a Shabbos meal with the Glazerson family*, I thought. I was beginning to call Bayit Vegan the "who's who column."

That Shabbos, I sat marveling at Rabbi Glazerson's brilliance. Mrs. Glazerson possessed a remarkable gift of asking stimulating, thought-provoking questions. Shmuel gave a *devar Torah* as well; it was so spiritually enriched that Channah had to ask him to slow down and speak in English so that we could both follow.

After dinner that night I told her how happy I was that I was not the only one who hadn't understood. She smiled. "Shmuel gets so excited about the parashah that I always have to ask him to put on the brakes a little, so I can have time to absorb what he's expounding."

From the example of this couple, infused with the inner strength that comes from a Torah-based upbringing, I received strength myself. Through their acts of kindness, they were able to assist me in finding my own apartment – in close proximity to many of our mutual friends in Bayit Vegan.

The first time I walked through the doorway of my newly leased apartment, tears of joy sprang to my eyes. Softly, I said, "Thank God!"

My nerves were completely shattered after having spent a day with the movers, but I felt it was an opportune moment to recite my favorite *tehillim*. Suddenly serenity returned. Surveying my new quarters, I knew my antique sofa and chair would soon seem at home in the living room. I could envision the spiral bookcase filled with my Judaic books.

Standing in the doorway to the kitchen, I imagined how beautiful it would look with my beautiful set of kitchen towels. I pictured myself baking challah, making *cholent*, and cooking chicken soup. It was going to be big-time fun, learning all the new recipes! Gripped by a desire to continue the tradition of great Jewish cooking, I suddenly had a sobering thought: *This means observing kashrus!* The classroom scenarios were over; now it was time for hands-on training. I wondered whether I would need help making kugel for the first time. I had once thought I was a good cook! *Hadn't I told my friends that I would be cooking their favorite dishes as soon as I got settled? Oh, Ahuvah! There's lots of work to be done.*

I always keep a pencil and paper handy; writing is like therapy for me. Now, after the stress and excitement of moving day, I laughed as I flopped onto the sofa bed amongst the many boxes in the middle of the floor and began writing. My thoughts were on *b'nei Yisrael* and their forty years of wandering through the desert wilderness. The Torah records that *b'nei Yisrael* made forty-two stops before reaching the Promised Land. Since leaving my first seminary, I had already made seven moves within a four-month period; I began wondering what the next thirty-five would be like and where they would lead me.

Exploring the deeper side of my own wanderings, I realized that seven, according to the Torah, is the number that represents completion, as God created the world in seven days. I truly felt a sense of completion in my seventh abode. I wondered what the eighth would bring.

I was deeply indebted to the loving friends who had taken me into their homes like they would their own sister. Bayit Vegan is a cosmopolitan neighborhood. Its residents literally come from all over the globe. Thus, it is a reminder that the Jews are a universal people who are representative of the whole world. This international flavor contributed to my feeling at home. (In fact, the name means "Home and Garden.") I felt it was a home for all.

One Shabbos I was walking down Rechov Bayit Vegan to my apartment when a distinguished-looking gentleman dressed in black with a long white beard and tallis walked over to me and said, "Excuse me, Ms. Gray. Where are you from?" (After four years in Bayit Vegan, I had become a familiar sight to the established residents.)

"Chicago," I said, startled.

"Then who was it who comes from Mississippi?"

"That was my parents and grandparents. They were from Mound Bayou, Mississippi."

"Well, I am from Boyle, Mississippi."

I was stunned.

"Have you heard of Boyle, Ms. Gray?"

"Yes. It's near my father's birthplace, Merrigold."

He pointed to an apartment on Rechov Bayit Vegan. "My wife and I live there; please come by and visit us some time."

I continued to walk back to my apartment, thinking, *This is unbelievable. Who would have ever believed that a chareidi rabbi in Bayit Vegan was raised in the same state as my father!*

Since then, I have been a Shabbos guest at the home of Rabbi Abraham Weiner and his wife, Rochel Leah. Curious about the type of relationship that existed between Blacks and Jews in those days, I asked the rabbi.

"Jews and Blacks had a very close relationship in my hometown, and I had a Negro nanny," he told me. "Her family and mine were very close."

When I left their home I meditated on Rabbi Weiner's words describing the closeness between our two people. How I yearned for the coming of Mashiach who would herald in peace and harmony among Jews and gentiles alike.

The overwhelming majority of Bayit Vegan's residents are observant Jews, but within that stratum of traditional religious observance lies a highly pluralistic community. In a short walk down any street in Bayit Vegan, one will encounter a mother with anywhere up to eight or ten children tagging along. Perhaps you'll also see one of the many elderly citizens, often accompanied by a nurse tending to her patient's needs. A little further, you may see a group of *yeshivah bachurim* racing to the local felafel or pizza shop during their lunch hour. "Street-talk" will often be spiced with a *devar Torah*, distinguishing this neighborhood from others nearby. If you care to eavesdrop you will often pick up Hebrew, English in a large variety of accents, and Yiddish. You can also hear German, French, Polish, or Russian.

Many residents have university degrees; in fact, there are a number of internationally renowned scientists living in the neighborhood. Should one wish to prepare a listing of authors of books, they can expect to find a relatively large number living in Bayit Vegan. In addition, it has been the base of some of the most prominent names in the Orthodox world. On every street one can find scores of places of learning and prayer.

My friendships in Bayit Vegan have continued to grow and mature. Each family that invited me to eat with them for Shabbos would introduce me to another. The process personified the verse in the Book of *Mishlei*: "A man with friends is befriended!" (18:24).

The Beers made this networking process easy for me right from the beginning. Rabbi and Rebbetzin Beer had lived in Bayit Vegan for twenty-nine years. They knew next to everyone and were highly respected in the neighborhood. Once I had gotten settled, Chaya Beer recommended that I visit all the different synagogues in the area to see where I would feel most at home on Shabbos and Jewish holidays. I compared my search for a shul to shopping for a brand-new pair of shoes; first you have to try them on and then you have to walk around in them a while to make sure they are perfectly comfortable for your feet. I finally chose the Gra shul, the largest shul in Bayit Vegan, with services conducted according to the Ashkenazi tradition. I felt more at home there than in any other shul. My shul was much more than a place where I prayed — it was the beginning of a new *derech* for me.

On Shabbos I was privileged to sit with Rebbetzin Heyman on my left, Rebbetzin Chaya Beer on her left, and Rebbetzin Carmell next to her. As time progressed, I became better acquainted with Rebbetzin Carmell. Every Shabbos morning, I felt I was sitting next to women who were like our esteemed matriarchs, Sarah, Rivkah, Rachel, and Leah.

I also visited Avraham and Rochel Schwartzbaum on a regular basis. I vividly remember one occasion, a few years before their youngest son Yudie's bar mitzvah. We had just finished another lovely meal, complete with Rochel's luscious homemade challah. After giving his *devar Torah*, Avraham asked Yudie if he had anything to say. Yudie shyly gave a *devar Torah*, and we all congratulated him.

Later, while Yudie was clearing the table, I whispered to Rochel, "He's brilliant!"

Rochel whispered back, "Ahuvah, this is the first time he's given a *devar Torah* when we had a guest."

"I guess I'm not a guest anymore," I responded happily.

Sukkos is the holiday that commemorates the Jewish people's forty years of wandering in the desert. It is a lovely time for bringing people together. The Schwartzbaums invited me for one of the holiday meals, where I was blessed with meeting a very modest couple, Rabbi Yaakov and Sheila Iskowitz. Rabbi Iskowitz had served for twenty years as chaplain in the U.S. Army, and their home had often served as a "halfway-house" for soldiers and wayfarers. Reb Yaakov credits his wife's *cholent*, instead of his own teaching talent, with bringing unlearned Jews further along the road to observance of the Jewish tradition.

One evening, when engaged in a joyous conversation in the Beers' sukkah about how each of us had spent Sukkos in previous years, the Beers introduced me to the Frohweins — a very special family who had recently moved to Bayit Vegan from England.

If one could give an award for the most accommodating host and hostess, James and Tonia would have to be one of the first couples to qualify for it! In the Frohwein home I experienced the etiquette of the British firsthand. Their desire is to make their guests feel really at home, always ensuring that everyone has plenty to eat and drink. They really spoil you!

Tonia, a descendant of the Baal Shem Tov, always had thought-provoking remarks to make on the parashah. A natural teacher, she had us all sitting on the edge of our seats. Tirtsa, their daughter, was born in London and had studied at Gateshead, the famous English center of Jewish learning. She and I discovered that we were both enamored with Rabbi Akiva Tatz's masterpiece *Living Inspired*. I had read it ten times; I think Tirtsa was on her twelfth.

I was receiving Shabbos invitations months in advance, and it became common knowledge in the neighborhood, "If you'd like Ahuvah over as a guest, you'll have to book ahead!" By now, I had kind of a rotation schedule for Shabbos with the various families that I frequented. I was also starting to receive invitations to visit other neighborhoods.

But no matter how beautiful and scenic the other areas were, I was always extremely happy to come back to Bayit Vegan. Whenever I was leaving the neighborhood for Shabbos, I always made efforts to advise Rebbetzin Heyman and the Beers of my plans. I knew that they would be looking for me the next day in shul. I was so happy that Hashem had placed me under the protective umbrella of people who loved me and were so encouraging.

The home of Reb Tuvia and Chaya Heller was a regular stop on my Shabbos rotation. I was greatly inspired by their five daughters, with their singing, dancing, and love of Judaism in the spirit of the Chassidic tradition. They invited me to the bas mitzvah of their daughter Nechama, held at Rachel's Tomb. The last time I had visited that site I was there as a Christian. This time I was there as an observant Jew.

I immediately felt at home with the Sherils, who had made aliyah from England, giving up Daniel's prosperous medical practice there to start over in Eretz Yisrael.

My circle of friends continued to increase as well as my love and respect for Judaism. Becoming a Jew taught me *savlanut*, patience, and a new definition of sincerity. Whatever we did for each other was from the heart. Whenever I tried to express my appreciation and gratitude for acts of kindness, my friends would simply say, "*Ein davar* (it's nothing). It's a mitzvah, Ahuvah! Hashem loves the *ger*. We learned how to treat our guests from Avraham Avinu."

With deep gratitude I would thank Hashem for having created His loving child. I had identified with Avraham Avinu since I was a child and now was reaping the benefit of his greatness. Once during Rebbetzin Henkin's Chumash class we read a *midrash* about Avraham Avinu's unlimited hospitality, how he had always run to meet his guests and escort them. I began to cry because I knew people just like that.

Spending much time in other people's houses leaves me in awe of religious Jewish women. Our homes are a daily sanctification of the Name of Hashem. I came from a fine family. I saw love and kindness and devotion to the poor, and I was raised with values of strict morality and refinement. Yet when I enter a Torah home, the daily, moment-to-moment sanctification of God's Name that I experience far surpasses anything that I was raised with.

It was a long and often painful road that brought me to Jerusalem and to the understanding that I was willing to give up everything to become a part of the Jewish people. To me, the doorway of our Jewish home is an entrance to a sanctuary. My soul found a dwelling place in the Torah home; it is like a shelter from the outside world. The sanctity of the Torah home permeates the religious community and it doesn't exist outside of *Yiddishkeit*.

I marvel at the Jewish woman's attitude toward the family. In the beginning I wondered, *How would I ever be able to manage all those responsibilities: a husband, career, davening, and the halachos of Shabbos?* Week after week as I was invited into homes, I realized that the Jewish woman provides the physical and spiritual substance for her family and home, the sanctuary.

The hospitality of the Jewish people continued to amaze me as I met more and more families. I felt honored to be a guest of Rabbi Aryeh Carmell, *shlita*, and Rebbetzin Carmell. Rav Carmell, originally from England, is distinguished in the Jewish world as a teacher and author and renowned as an authority on *mussar* and Rabbi Dessler's works. He has an excellent way of teaching the weekly parashah. After lunch he takes out a *chumash*, has each of us read the text in Hebrew, and then translates it into English.

Sitting at the Carmells' table, I remembered a lesson I had learned in seminary: The table represents the sacrificial altar, and therefore it is regarded as holy to observant Jews. During the spiritually elevating Shabbos with Rabbi Carmell, I could actually feel the holiness.

Sometimes good things come in packages. At one exceptional Shabbos lunch, the well-known author and scientist Professor Cyril Domb was also the Carmells' guest. The professor's wife, Shirley, was in London visiting her mother. My only regret was that I couldn't tape the *divrei Torah*. It was a once-in-a-lifetime opportunity to be at a Shabbos table together with such knowledgeable men, where Rabbi Carmell's scholarly approach to the Torah and Professor Domb's scientific knowledge would be combined. I was speechless throughout their entire discourse.

I've often wondered what my life would have been like if I had had a father like Rabbis Emanuel and Aaron Feldman. Both are Talmudic scholars residing in Bayit Vegan, sons of the famous scholar Rabbi Joseph H. Feldman, *zt"l*. Rabbi Emanuel Feldman, *shlita*, is well known in the religious community as the editor of *Tradition* magazine. I enjoy the brilliant and lively discussions at the Shabbos table with his wife and family.

Rabbi Feldman often spoke of his brother Aaron, and I longed to finally meet the author of *The River, the Kettle and the Bird*. Finally, I was invited to spend a Shabbos with Rabbi and Rebbetzin Aaron Feldman. Rabbi Feldman was the dean at Yeshivas Beer HaTorah and Rebbetzin Feldman was the housemother at Neve Yerushalayim Seminary. That was my opportunity to ask the question that I had pondered in my heart for so long: Why had I not been born to a Jewish family? Rabbi Feldman told me that I was probably better off the way I had come into Judaism, as a *ger tzeddek*. Because I came with a "fresh eye" and sincerity, I would be less likely to take the Torah for granted.

After that first wonderful visit I kept going back. It wasn't just on account of the homemade challah and *cholent*, even though they were exceptional. Rather, it was for the *shalom bayis* — the peace and tranquility in that home! I found the Feldmans to be very warm and the rabbi's great sense of humor enhanced my visits.

I was particularly excited because I could ask Rabbi Feldman about any verse in the Tanach and he would explain the meaning. Once I asked him, "Rabbi Feldman, do you know what was meant by the prophet Michah, 'He has told you, man, what is good and what the Lord requires of you: only to do justice, to love kindness, and to walk humbly with your God'?"

Rabbi Feldman answered, "Our Sages say that the key to understanding the Torah and the six hundred and thirteen mitzvos rests upon the three things contained in this verse. Firstly, to do justice: mankind must live according to law. Second, to love kindness, which is *chesed*, having compassion. Finally, to walk humbly with God speaks of modesty.

"Was this one of your favorite verses, Ahuvah?"

"Yes, Rabbi Feldman, I used to walk around quoting *Michah* 6:8 all day long!"

"You certainly chose a good one, Ahuvah."

Imagine, Rabbi Feldman complimenting me. My confidence rose to another level.

"You know," he continued, "the entirety of the Torah is based on these three things."

Walking home I felt satisfied, not only from the Shabbos delicacies, but from the soul-nourishing food that I had ingested. I said quietly, "Thank You, God, for placing me around such loving and knowledgeable people."

I have lived in Bayit Vegan for five years now. I am getting acquainted with more and more families while my established friendships are growing richer all the time. It has been such a privilege to be invited into such special homes, week after week.

The families whom I have mentioned, and many more whose names did not find their way into this work, have been the source of my strength. There is no way I can personally express my gratitude to all of them. Even in writing the words seem grossly inadequate as I attempt to express the true essence of the love they have shown me.

Chapter 12

To Be a Jew

January 2, 2000. Ruth and I positioned ourselves at the podium at the Israel Center in Jerusalem before a crowd of two hundred plus.

"The woman I'm standing next to this evening is no longer the same woman I met seven years ago," Ruth, my partner and long-time friend through much of my spiritual journey, introduced me at a lecture entitled "Two Paths, One Vision." "I knew her as Delores Gray. She is now Ahuvah Gray. But she didn't just change her name; she changed her birthright."

My mind again traversed the path that I had traveled. I began speaking. "Often at my lectures I am asked what were the spiritual dynamics that caused me to make such a radical metamorphosis. We are taught that before the Torah was given at Sinai, Hashem went to all the other nations and offered the Torah to them. Even though the majority of each nation refused it, the Vilna Gaon says there were souls among those nations that did desire the Torah. I believe that I am a *gilgul* of one of those *neshamos*. I am still amazed myself."

Ruth then spoke about the effect of my conversion on her, a nonobservant Jew. "Our friendship forces me to constantly reexamine my commitment. A convert gives us a chance to see things through a child's eyes: you don't know what you have until somebody else wants it."

People surrounded us at the close of the lecture, each one brimming with questions. One of them, who introduced herself as Sarah, asked me about seminary life.

"I was fifty-one years old when I started studying at a *chareidi* institution," I began. "I was old enough to be the mother of most of the girls there, but instead we were like sisters. They gave me such *chizuk*.

"Four of us in particular developed a very close rapport. Stacey from Atlanta, Stephanie from Brazil, Amanda from London, and I. Boy, what a team. We had such great times together. Even though we were in different classes, we made sure to have lunch together — that was our time for shmoozing. Whenever I gave a lecture, the 'inner circle' was always there with me. I never felt alone." Then I posed a question of my own: "Sarah, have you ever attended a seminary?"

"No, Ahuvah. I am afraid I am too old now."

I laughed. "Remember, I was fifty when I started."

Sarah then had a more sensitive question for me. "Ahuvah, have you ever encountered any difficulties living in a *chareidi* neighborhood?"

This was one I was glad to answer. "I've been totally accepted by the entire community. My *rebbetzin* has been sitting in the front row this evening; she attends every lecture she possible can.

"I can't say that my path has been without obstacles. Critics of Torah-observant Jews sometimes ask me if I found problems with Judaism. 'On the contrary,' I answer them, 'with traditional Judaism I feel like a complete person.' I turned to Orthodox Judaism because my *neshamah* felt its *sheleimus* at its highest level there. Judaism is like a rare delicacy. If you're invited to a gourmet meal, why settle for something less?" At this point Sarah gave me a nod of approval.

"What hurts me deeply are the warring fractions within Judaism. Nothing gives me greater satisfaction than seeing the Jewish people when they are united; it's a true *kiddush Hashem*. The most amazing thing to me has been the loving reverence and awe that Jews have for the Name of God. Since I've lived in Bayit Vegan, I have never heard anyone use God's Name superficially! In the spirit of our tradition, Jewish people don't use Hashem's Name superficially. This is rare, Sarah. I don't think it exists in any other religion.

"I remember the first time I saw a religious Jew dressed in black. I said out loud, 'Oh my goodness, that man is holy!' I had read in the Bible about Avraham, and I thought that Avraham must have looked something like that. That was the imagination of a thirteen-year-old Black girl!

"I've often wondered where the Jewish people get the stamina to persevere when surrounded by anti-Semitism all over the world. I believe it is innate. The Jews are called 'k'shei oref,' a stubborn people. Hashem has placed in every Jew a coping mechanism — obstinacy. Throughout the horrors of the Crusades, the Spanish Inquisition, pogroms, and the Holocaust, the Jewish people continue to exist and thrive.

"What is the purpose of all this suffering? The answer lies in the Divine promise to Avraham that he would inherit the Land of Israel. The Jew is given the Land of Israel as the base for his spiritual mission, and he is not supposed to feel comfortable in the Diaspora. I believe that this is one reason why anti-Semitism exists:

to remind the Jew that he's a *Yid* and that he has a homeland. If we as Jews want to hasten the coming of Mashiach, we should all come home. Not only physically, but also spiritually. Coming home in the full sense entails returning to Torah and to view commitment to it as a moral obligation and responsibility to one's fellow Jews.

"Sarah, I have chosen to live a Torah life based upon the six hundred and thirteen mitzvos, according to the written law and the oral law that were given over to Moshe at Sinai and transmitted in an unbroken chain to us today. My rabbi was taught by his rabbi, and that rabbi was taught by his rabbi, and the teaching can be traced all the way back to Sinai. It is called *mesorah*.

"This is the beauty which I have found in Judaism. I have found my spiritual roots. They have a beginning, and I like that beginning. I became a Jew because I want to live out my days according to the Divine law that was given to Moshe at Mount Sinai, which hasn't changed until today. It is still intact. It's a *berachah* to be among people who conduct their lives in this manner."

To conclude, I shared with Sarah and the others one of my most cherished Torah stories. "I have always loved the story of Rus. During the time of my conversion, I thought about it frequently. That brief exchange between Naomi and her two daughters-in-law was extremely poignant. Both women expressed their feelings as they stood weeping by the roadside with Naomi. Orpah loved Naomi greatly, and she genuinely did not want to part from her. Nevertheless, she turned back. Rus, on the other hand, clung to her.

"Orpah became the great-grandmother of Golias, who blasphemed Hashem. Rus, on the other hand, became the great-grandmother of King David, the antithesis of Golias. What did

Rus have that Orpah didn't? It was the strength of character to be faithful to one's convictions. Orpah didn't have the strength to substantiate her emotions. She lacked the stamina to put the totality of her being behind her beliefs.

"You know what makes a Jew a good Jew? It's more than a feeling. Feelings may change. Feelings don't give the ability to carry out a rational decision. My ability to persevere comes through prayer. It's like this: Hashem gave me a Jewish *neshamah*; that makes me a *Yid*. However, if I want to be a Jew, I have to daven, study the Torah, and do mitzvos. In the final analysis, it really doesn't matter what my mother, father, sister, or brothers think. In the end this thing is just between God and me."

Chapter 13

She Works Hard for the Money

andle clutched in my detergent-scoured hand, I searched the nooks and crannies of my Bayit Vegan apartment for the smallest sign of one of the great peculiarities of God's creation – *chametz*. In the light of the shimmering candlelight I peered down at my hands, chuckling to myself as I thought about what my siblings would say: "You want to be like Princess Grace? With working-class hands like these, Prince Rainier will never want to marry you!"

My search concluded, I wrapped the remnants of the ubiquitous *chametz* in newspaper, and then declared any *chametz* that had yet eluded the scan of my quickly drooping eyelids to be ownerless like the dust of the earth.

How will I ever sit up until midnight at the Frohweins' seder tomorrow night? I wondered.

One of my first *ulpan* lessons popped into my exhausted head: "*Ein li koach, ein li moach!*" I considered this. *Right now I feel that I have neither strength nor brains, and for someone who has worked as hard as I have for a quarter of a century, I'm awfully poor, but, baruch Hashem, there is one thing I can lay claim to – peace.* After I had called it a day, the words of the bedtime prayer, *HaMapil*, slowly rolled off my lips: "May it be Your will, Hashem, my God and the God of my forefathers, that You lay me down to sleep in peace and raise me erect in peace."

It was *erev Pesach* and finally the closing stages of one of the most physically taxing months in my life had arrived.

When I moved to Israel, the question of what I was going to do for a livelihood had not occurred to me. I was studying Torah and learning Hebrew. Satisfying as that was, the reality of how to support myself soon stared me in the face.

I explored the various alternatives available to an "Anglo-Saxon" (as English-speakers are called in Israel). Because I was studying at the seminary, I wanted something local, if possible. What I discovered was that I could earn more money by cleaning houses than by utilizing my sales and marketing skills. My sister thought I was nuts! "Do you mean to tell me you left a job making three thousand dollars a month and closed down your travel agency to move to Israel to clean houses? That's crazy!"

The word spread quickly in Bayit Vegan that I was cleaning houses. The families that I worked for always said, "Ahuvah, you do such a thorough job." How grateful I was to my beloved mother for forcing me to clean when all my friends were out playing on the weekends. My objective in operating the cleaning service was to give house-cleaning a personal touch; I tried to clean each person's home as if it was my own. The result was that I had more work than I could manage, and I eventually hired four workers to help ease the burden. With Pesach not far off, my timing was perfect.

Even though my mother had taught us to clean very meticulously, this Pesach cleaning was not to be believed! In the kitchen, I was asked to use a needle and toothpick to get the dirt out of corners. I later found out at seminary that the primary objective was to eliminate *chametz*, as opposed to dirt, but many times it was difficult to differentiate between the two.

After my first exercise in Pesach-cleaning, I thought there had to be a better way to do it. Why not incorporate the Pesach-cleaning into the weekly cleaning for Shabbos? I discussed my plan with a few of my clients, and they liked the idea. The following Pesach I was better prepared and less tired by the time the seder came around. But even so, it was still very exhausting. I asked Chaya Beer the obvious question: "How can I enjoy this holiday when I am so tired?"

She said, "Ahuvah, when we sit down tonight for Pesach, Jews all over the world will be sitting down together. This united feeling should fortify you with renewed vigor."

Every year, as I sit down at the seder table to eat the "poor man's bread" (as it is called in the Haggadah), I remember Chaya Beer's words. In unity there is strength!

My appetite for hard work didn't just appear; it came as a legacy from my forebears. My granddaddy, my mother's father, Willie Franklin, placed the greatest importance on working hard and providing for his family. In those days, life was a struggle for survival for African-Americans. My mother and all of my aunts and uncles all started out as blue-collar workers, but over the years they worked their way up to the upper middle class. In fact, we have two aunts and two uncles who became millionaires. How they did it in those restrictive times never ceases to amaze me. I have always been extremely proud of them. I used them as role models when I was lecturing to youth groups. "Grandparents lay the foundations and hold families together by their example," I would tell the youngsters.

When I was four years old, my granddaddy would sit me on his knee and say, "My word is my bond. Little Delores, if a person can't trust your word, he can't trust you." Now I am fifty-four years old, living in Jerusalem, and I can still hear the echo of Granddaddy's voice giving me the first possible *mussar* lesson I ever received in my life. As a result of his positive stalwart teaching on commitment, I do all I can to keep my word to this very day.

Granddaddy had never taken a piano or guitar lesson in his life, but he could play every musical instrument by ear. He also built his home with his own hands. He personified the Black manhood of that era. I grew up saying, "I want to marry a man who will build me a house, just like my granddaddy."

Lelar Franklin, my grandmother, with her beautiful brown skin, high cheekbones, and keen nose looked like a princess. She grew up near the Mississippi Gulf and New Orleans, daughter of a Black mother who died when she was young and Colonel Funches, a Native American who worked as a scout for the U.S. Army.

When I worked for Continental as flight attendant, I used to fly eight Los Angeles turnarounds a month. After marrying, I was promoted to flight attendant supervisor. This position involved scheduling flight attendants for flights when someone called in sick, counseling, responsibility for proper grooming before a flight, weighing-in female flight attendants to ensure they met the weight requirements, and much more.

I became a jack-of-all-trades. When the girls decided to marry, I became a marriage counselor. When they were sick, I became a doctor: "Yes, I agree with you. If you feel you are catching a cold, you should stay home. You could get an ear-block."

When the counseling started to become involved, I would always give my Grandmother Franklin a call. Grandmother never held a paying job and had not more than a grade school education. Yet she was one of the wisest women I have ever known. She used to tell me, "Delores, we aren't college educated, but we have mother-wit."

"What's that?" I'd ask her.

She would answer, "It is God-given sense; it comes from God."

The stories from my days as a flight attendant supervisor are too numerous to detail in this book. However, one that I would like to share is about Tom Smith (not his actual name). Tom was White and brought up in the South. On a couple of occasions when I had to counsel him, I perceived that no matter how tactful I was, he was still uncomfortable with our discussions. The last confrontation I had with Tom was over a complaint letter. The passenger claimed that Tom had treated him rudely when he asked for a second beverage, giving him a sharp retort. This was one type of incident which I could not overlook.

Since it was my policy not to upset a flight attendant before a flight, I asked Tom if he would stop by my office when he returned from his next flight. He wasn't thrilled about the idea, but he agreed.

Once in my office, Tom denied the entire incident. I offered him the letter to read. Afterwards, I explained to him that I had no choice but to put the letter in his file. He wasn't at all pleased with my decision, and the meeting ended by my assuring him that I only had his best interests at heart.

Afterwards, I discussed the entire episode with my grand-mother. "Grandmother, I think the problem wasn't really the complaint letter. The problem was I am Black and a female. He is not used to being subordinate to a woman. I am sure that it was very difficult for him, but I was as tactful as I could be."

My grandmother said, "Give him time. One day he will real-ize that you were really trying to help him keep his job."

Following this incident, Tom transferred to the flight atten-dant base in Houston. A few months later, I was advised that he had been terminated. About six months later I received the loveli-est letter from Tom. The letter stated that he was sorry that he had behaved so poorly. He finally realized after his termination that our many counseling sessions were only meant to help him. He thanked me for being so considerate of his feelings. I took the letter home and read it to my grandmother, and we cried to-gether.

Several months later, I turned to Grandmother once again. "Grandmother, one of my flight attendants gave me some confi-dential information. She explained that she told me about it only because she feels more comfortable with me than with anyone else. My base manager called me in and demanded to know the nature of our conversation, but I told her that the flight attendant had shared the information confidentially. The manager threat-ened me with my job for withholding the information. I held firm; I told her I respect her position, but it would be a breach of trust if I disclosed the nature of our meeting. Grandmother, did I do the right thing?"

"Yes, Delores, you acted very professionally and true to your convictions," I was told. "She wasn't really going to fire you; it was a bluff. When you stood up to her, she withdrew her threat. If she's a reasonable, intelligent person, she won't try this again."

Again, as always, I marveled at her wisdom.

After leaving Neve, I took an eighteen-month tour guide course with Archeological Seminar, Ltd. It was a very demanding course, and when it drew to a close I felt both elated and sad — elated because I would have a life of my own again and sad because I had developed some very close relationships.

We had some wonderful examples of model students. Rabbi Ken Spiro, a staff member of Aish HaTorah's Discovery program, was a walking historian. Asher Orbit was an expert on geology and the water systems throughout Israel. Esti Herskowitz mothered all of us. She invited me for Shabbos, and arranged personal study sessions for me at her husband's office, drilling me like a sergeant to help me prepare for the oral examination.

One summer day after I had graduated, I was giving a tour in the Old City when I heard a familiar voice. It was Esti. She was giving a tour later that day for Aish HaTorah. I was scheduled to lecture for the same group the following night. When I arrived the next evening they gave me warm regards from Esti and raved about their tour. What a small world we live in!

Becoming a tour guide has given me a marvelous opportunity to show people this Holy Land. It is also a mitzvah to share the history of this special country with others. I meet many different people from various backgrounds, some of whom make a deep impression on me.

Chapter 14

Keep Smiling

My journey has had many stops along the way: Chicago, Mound Bayou, Los Angeles, and, finally, Jerusalem. Things did not come easily – good things never do – but there have been bright spots all along, smiles, friendships, caring people. These are just a few of those wonderful moments that kept me smiling.

On the eighteenth of Elul, 1998, I finished writing my book. After *Selichos* and *shacharis*, I gave a sigh of relief. I had just completed fifty-two years of my life, and it was all written in those chapters. What a pleasure to complete my book. And how appropriate to do it in Elul. Elul, the twelfth and last month of the Jewish calendar, is a month of both culmination and preparation. In Elul we examine our behavior and actions of the previous twelve months while we prepare resolutions which will bring us to a better and richer fulfillment of the year to come. The closing of each year is comparable to the writing of our own autobiography, with the chapters of our lives written annually in our own books.

Eager to share the good news, I called my friend Shaina Medwed. "Ahuvah, that's great! Do you know what today is? It's the birthday of the Baal Shem Tov and the Baal HaTanya, and also the *yahrtzeit* of the Maharal. See to whom you are spiritually at-tuned!" Her words gladdened my heart; I simply couldn't stop smiling.

With the closing of the old year and the ushering in of the new, the holidays flew by. It was already Simchas Torah. Custom-arily a rabbi in the congregation is given the honor of being "*chasan Torah*," making the blessing at the conclusion of the yearly cycle of Torah readings. Rabbi Leib Heyman, the rabbi of the Gra, was honored with *chasan Torah*. Professor Leo Levi was awarded "*chasan Bereishis*," making the *berachah* on the first para-shah of the new year. Both men, again following tradition, later made a *kiddush* to mark the event.

Miriam Levi made their *kiddush* in their home. It was a joy-ous event and done in fine taste. Typical of the Levis' health-conscious cuisine, we were served delicious organic vegetables, scrumptious hors d'oeuvres, and sugarless pastries. It was my first time attending such a *kiddush*; truly a memorable occasion, with almost the entire congregation stopping by to wish *mazal tov* and show the customary respect due.

Rabbi Heyman's *kiddush* was held a few weeks later at the Gra shul. In her usual manner, Rebbetzin Heyman greeted every-one with a smile as she hurried to offer her guests kugel and her special herring. Just watching her made me feel exhausted! When she finally made her way over to our table, I couldn't contain my-self. "Rebbetzin," I said, "when I grow up I want to be just like you!" I began to laugh, and Shaina Malka, the *rebbetzin*'s daugh-ter, Chaya Beer, and Shaina Medwed all joined in.

Though it was a warm and funny moment, there was a seri-ous side to my words: In essence, I was saying that when I reached her level of spiritual maturity I hoped that, with God's help, I would follow her example of a gracious hostess — and perhaps even have some level of her Torah knowledge!

There were other incidents that kept me smiling through the years. I used to clean the Beers' house for Shabbos while I was still in the process of converting. Chaya took the opportunity to teach me about keeping a Torah home as we worked together. It was a guided tour in Judaism! Once, on the Thursday before Pesach, I had just finished the job and sat down to eat lunch with the Beers. After we'd eaten, Rabbi Beer turned to me, "Ahuvah," he said, "I am going to pay you for next week. But you cannot work during the holiday because as far as we are concerned you are Jewish."

I was in tears again, and Chaya said, "Ahuvah, stop that. We thank Hashem for you every day. Come to us for one of the *yom tov* meals, you hear?"

When I left, I was smiling. Walking home I thought, *Whatever I go through in Bayit Vegan, I don't have to suffer through it alone.*

Another wonderful memory, again connected to a *yom tov,* this time Shavuos:

I had just returned from the Shavuos evening service in the Gra synagogue. Though I'd lived in Israel for four years, much to my frustration I still couldn't understand the *devar Torah* that Rabbi Heyman had given in Hebrew. Fortunately, my host for the evening, Dr. Sheril, davened in the same shul and was eager to share the Torah thought.

"Rabbi Heyman spoke about Rus," he told me, "the most famous of converts. He related her journey to that of all converts and to *Tehillim.* The book of Psalms, Rabbi Heyman said, brings comfort to the many different people of the world. Rabbi Heyman actually mentioned a non-Jewish woman who had taught her children and grandchildren the twenty-third Psalm."

I could barely contain myself. "Dr. Sheril, pardon me for interrupting, but did Rabbi Heyman mention the name of the woman?"

Dr. Sheril didn't recall if the *rav* had mentioned the name of the woman.

The next morning I could hardly wait to speak to Rebbetzin Heyman. "Ahuvale, dear," she answered my eager question, "of course it was about you and your grandmother. He didn't mention you by name because he didn't want to embarrass you!"

The *rebbetzin* went on to tell me the rest of the *rav's vort*. "In our own neighborhood," he'd said, "we have a genuine *giyores*, a righteous convert. This remarkable woman was taught the twenty-third psalm by her grandmother at the age of four. Her grandmother would read psalms to the sick and elderly in her town in Mississippi. The *giyores's* mother used to feed and care for the sick and homeless in her own home. With such role models our friend grew to maturity, with her love and admiration of the Book of Psalms growing, too. She recited Tehillim daily — until her love for the Almighty grew so strong that she felt compelled to convert to Judaism.

"This *giyores* is an example of how *Tehillim* and the coming of Mashiach relate to each other. Rus joined the Jewish people and became the great-grandmother of King David, who wrote *sefer Tehillim* through which he brought so many to believe in the one God. We know from the tradition of our Sages that after Mashiach comes no more converts will be accepted, but here we have one who made it in the merit of her grandmother."

"What a beautiful legacy for my grandmother," I murmured, with tears in my eyes. "Can you imagine? My grandmother, daughter of sharecroppers, could end up making it to the Gra shul in Jerusalem on Shavuos eve? What a great honor for her!"

As I walked to lunch I felt myself speaking to my grandmother once again. "Grandmother, you never cease to amaze me. You have come from Mound Bayou, Mississippi, all the way to Jerusalem — all in the merit of the Psalms."

Chapter 15

Tishah B'Av through the Eyes of a Convert

ugust 2, 1998. Four years had elapsed since I had first observed the fast of Tishah B'Av. The meaning of the portentous events of Tishah B'Av of 1994 still plagued me. The most amazing thing about the entire incident was that though I felt the pain of the day deeply, at the time I had no idea whatsoever that I was going to convert to Judaism.

I had posed the question to Yosef: "Why is the fast of Tishah B'Av so painful?"

This was his poignant answer:

"Tishah B'Av focuses on Israel as a nation. It forces the Jewish people to realize that our present world of exile is not the real world. We need to recall what we lost. When we had the Temple, the *Shechinah* – the Divine Presence – dwelt among us; when we lost the Temple because of our transgressions, the *Shechinah* left.

"The only way for the rest of mankind to know about holiness was for there to be an exile. With the exile of our people, the rest of the world was given an opportunity to learn about holiness. By means of sacred words and deeds – divine sparks – we were able to be a light to the nations, even in exile.

"However, before becoming a light to the nations, we first need to become a light to ourselves. Rabbi Samson Raphael Hirsch says that the mourning of Tishah B'Av is not a journey to the graveyard. The pain that we reexperience at Tishah B'Av is not an end in itself; it's to teach the 'child' so that when he returns to the 'classroom' he will be a better pupil. Exile is our classroom. There's an ingathering of the exiles now, Ahuvah — both physical and spiritual. Through the ingathering of all of our divine sparks, there's a rebuilding of the Temple in a spiritual sense.

"When we had the Holy Temple everyone saw the glory of God. Jews and righteous gentiles traveled for days to see the magnificence of King Solomon's Temple. Our Sages recorded that great miracles occurred there. In the abode of the Divine Presence, the laws of nature were transcended. All the worshiper used to crowd into the Temple area by the thousands. When they prostrated themselves, there was miraculously room for each man to bow down.

"The Temple was a place where the soul was rejuvenated. In both Temples there were fifteen stairs which were arranged in the shape of a semicircle and led to the Court of the Israelites. When the priests and Levites ascended the stairs they would sing the *Shirei HaMaalos*, the Songs of Ascent. Each song represented an ascent, whereby the *neshamah* was enabled to reach a higher level.

"When Jews traveled to Jerusalem on the *shalosh regalim*, the three pilgrim festivals, each one was treated royally. The Jews of Jerusalem would open their homes for lodging to strangers and would feed their guests.

"Once our First and Second Temples were destroyed, we, the

Jewish people, did not only mourn the physical loss; we also mourned what we had lost of our spiritual heritage as a people. The Second Temple was destroyed because of *sinas chinam,* baseless hatred. We were made conscious of how much was lost. It was the closeness that the Jewish people once had one for another."

I could better comprehend the pain I associated with the fast of Tishah B'Av by remembering the pain of losing my mother. The loss of my mother exemplifies for me why the Jewish people mourn the loss of our Temple. Although I feel the pain of a great loss, it's a pain that dissipates when I think about the glory of God that was revealed through her life.

It's largely due to my great personal need for consolation that I have always loved the splendid words of Yeshayah, read on the Shabbos after Tishah B'av. Even when I was an ordained minister, I used to read this chapter of the Scriptures with tears in my eyes and wonder what the prophet meant when he said, "*Nachamu, nachamu* – Comfort, comfort my people..." (*Yeshayah* 40:1).

Through the eyes of a convert, I now know what it means to be comforted. Each of us, so to speak, has his own personal exile. Each exile carries with it a unique pain. Just as the Jewish people are in exile, so is a Jewish *neshamah* that resides inside a *ger;* just as the Jewish people long for their homeland, so does the Jewish *neshamah.* Once a potential convert has been exposed to Judaism and the Jewish people, that *neshamah* starts to crave for the Jewish life. My *neshamah* found its home in Bayit Vegan.

The words of the Psalmist beautifully reflect these feelings: "As the deer longs for brooks of water, so my soul longs for You, O God" (*Tehillim* 42:2). Rabbi Samson Raphael Hirsch compares this verse to the exiled Israel longing for God. So it was with my journey.

I wondered often why the journey of a *ger* had to be so painful. While I was in seminary I learned what the Sages taught: "It is a common thing for the life of a *ger* to be fraught with difficulties; one of the reasons is that the *ger* often waited a long time until he took steps to seek conversion." My rabbis explained the simple meaning of this: the moment he becomes convinced about the truth of Judaism, a person should not hesitate to move to action.

I realize that my pain comes from having been in exile so long. It was my past and not my present or my future that was the most painful for me. My family and my friends from my former life did not fully understood my quest, nor did they see the Glory of God that I am privileged to enjoy here in Jerusalem.

This rising of our spiritual hopes from the abyss of Tishah B'Av is what we experience as Jews on the first Shabbos of Tishah B'Av, the "Sabbath of Consolation." How fitting it is that the haftarah reading for that Shabbos is *Yeshayah*, ch. 40. Finally, a *ger tzeddek* is able to find rest and comfort from the loneliness and pain of the journey. When the Temple is rebuilt, multitudes of people will come to Jerusalem and see the *ger* comforted:

> *Let not the stranger who has joined himself to Hashem speak, saying, "Hashem will utterly separate me from His people"... And the strangers who join themselves to Hashem to serve Him and to love the Name of Hashem to become servants unto Him, all who guard the Sabbath against desecration, and grasp My covenant tightly – I will bring them to My holy mountain, and I will gladden them in My house of prayer. Their elevation-offerings and their feast-offerings will find favor on My Altar, for My House will be called a house of prayer for all the peoples. The*

word of my Lord, Hashem/Elokim, Who gathers in the dispersed of Israel: I shall gather to him even more than those already gathered to him.

(Yeshayah 51:3, 6–8)

What does it mean to mourn on Tishah B'Av? For me it means to see the future glory of Hashem when others don't mourn or perceive the present loss of the *Shechinah*. In this spirit we understand the Talmudic blessing: "*Kol hamisavel al Yerushalayim zocheh v'roeh b'simchasah* — Whoever mourns over Jerusalem is deserving to witness her joy."

I believe that we are able to experience in this lifetime, with God's help, a foretaste of the glory of the Third Temple and the World to Come. As a Jewess, I look forward to the day when all the different nations will see the glory of Hashem.

Epilogue

The fifteen chapters of this book correspond to the fifteen "Songs of Ascent" (*Tehillim*, ch. 120–134) which have been a major spiritual moving force for me all my life.

I finished writing this book during the month of Elul, a time when the Jewish people enter into personal introspection. Part of my own spiritual accounting has been to search my heart to ascertain that everything I have written here is factual and respects each person's viewpoint.

My dear friends, Shaina Medwed, author of *A Mother's Favorite Stories*, her husband, Dr. Medwed, and their son, Yitzchak, have been a constant source of strength and inspiration since the beginning of this book.

After I finished telling the Medweds about my mother and grandmother, Shaina told me, "Ahuvah, you should write a book."

"Shaina," I said, "I've known my entire life that I was going to write a book. I have a computer, but I don't have a printer."

My friend smiled at me and said, "What do you mean, a printer? Get busy, Ahuvah! I've written my entire book longhand."

To all future writers I would like to say, "Get busy!"

Glossary

a gutten erev Shabbos — happy Shabbos eve

Acharei Mos–Kedoshim — two Torah portions that are normally read together, except during a leap year

afikoman — a broken piece of matzah eaten at the end of the seder

Aharon — Aaron

Amorah — Gomorrah

Ashkenazi — characteristic of Jews from Eastern or Western Europe

Avinu — our patriarch

avos melachah — categories of work prohibited on the Sabbath

Avraham — Abraham

balagan — madhouse

baruch Hashem — thank God

bashert — predestined

Be'er Sheva — Beersheba

beis din — judicial court presided over by rabbis

beis midrash — place of study

berachah (pl. *berachos*) — blessing

b'nei Yisrael — the children of Israel

chag sameiach — happy holiday

challah — traditional bread served at Sabbath and holiday meals

chametz — leavened bread

Chanukah — Hanukkah, a Jewish holiday

chareidi — ultra-Orthodox

chavrusa — Torah learning partner

chesed — kindness

chizuk — strength, support

cholent — stew

Chumash — the five books of Moses

daven — pray

dayan (pl. *dayanim*) — judge

derech — path

devar Torah — a Torah discourse

Ein li koach, ein li moach — I have no strength, I have no brains

Eretz Yisrael — the Land of Israel

erev Pesach — the day before Pesach

felafel — a spicy dish, popular in the Middle East, of ground chick-
     peas formed into balls and fried

gebenched — blessed

ger — convert

ger tzeddek — righteous convert

gilgul — reincarnation

giyores — female convert

glatt kosher — kosher according to the strictest standards

Golias — Goliath

haftarah — portion from the Prophets or Writings read every
  Sabbath

Haggadah — prayer book containing the seder ritual

halachah — law

Hashem — God

hashgachah peratis — divine providence

Havdalah — the ceremony concluding the Sabbath

hechsher — symbol of kosher supervision

Ibn Ezra — a medieval commentator on the Torah

kabbalas Shabbos — prayers for the onset of Shabbos

kasher — to prepare meat or chicken in a way that will render it
  halachically permissible to eat

kashrus — dietary laws

kavanah — concentration

kedushah — holiness

kehunah — the priesthood of Aaron

Kiddush — a ceremonial blessing pronounced over wine at a Sabbath or holiday meal

kiddush – a party made on Sabbath after morning prayer services, usually to celebrate some special occasion

kohein (pl. *kohanim*) – male descendant of Aaron, the High Priest

kohein gadol – high priest

Koheles – Ecclesiastes

kugel – a tradition Jewish food made of potatoes, noodles, or vegetables

lashon hara – harmful or negative speech

l'chaim – a toast, "to life"

machzor – holiday prayer book

mah pitom – what is this?

Mashiach – the Messiah

mazal – fate, destiny

mazal tov – congratulations

mechitzah – separation, division

Megillas Rus – the Book of Ruth

meshugah – crazy

mezuzah – a parchment scroll bearing the verses of Shema and affixed to every doorpost

midrash – a story from the Oral Torah

mikveh – ritual pool

min haShamayim – Heaven sent

Mishlei – Proverbs

Mishneh Torah – Maimonides's Code of Jewish law

mitzvah (pl. mitzvos) — commandment

mizrach — east, the direction to which Jews traditionally face when praying

Modeh Ani — prayer said upon rising in the morning

Moshe — Moses

mussar — ethics

neshamah (pl. *neshamos*) — soul

niggun — melody

Noachide Laws — the laws given to Noah which all mankind is obligated to observe

Orpah — Orpha

parashah — a section of the Torah assigned for weekly reading

pareve — made without meat, milk, or their derivatives

plotzed — fainted

Rambam — Maimonides, a medieval commentator on the Oral Torah

Rashi — a medieval commentator on the Torah

rebbetzin — rabbi's wife

rechov — street

Rosh HaShanah — the Jewish New Year

Rus — Ruth

Sanhedrin — supreme court of Jewish law

shlep — drag

seder — a ritual meal held on the first (and second) night of

Passover to commemorate the Exodus

Sedom – Sodom

Selichos – repentance prayers

Sephardic – characteristic of Jews from Spain or Portugal

seudah – meal

seudah shelishis – the third Sabbath meal

Shabbos (pl. Shabbosos) – the Sabbath

shacharis – morning prayers

shalom – hello; goodbye; peace

Shamayim – Heaven

shanah tovah – have a good year

Shavuos – a Jewish holiday commemorating the giving of the Torah

sheleimus – completeness

Shemirath Shabbath – a book about Sabbath laws

Shemoneh Esrei – daily silent prayer

Shemos – the Book of Exodus

shiur – lecture

shivah – the seven-day mourning period

shlita – may he live long years

shmoozing – chatting

shofar – ram's horn

shul – synagogue

siddur — prayer book

siman tov u'mazal tov — congratulations and blessings

simanim — symbols

Simchas Torah — the last day of Sukkos, a celebration of the Torah

sukkah (pl. sukkos) — a booth with a roof of branches or leaves built for the holiday of Sukkos

Sukkos — a holiday celebrated in the fall, immediately after Yom Kippur

tallis (pl. talleisim) — prayer shawl

Tanach — the Jewish Bible, the Torah (the Five Books of Moses, the Prophets, and the Writings)

Tehillim — Psalms

teshuvah — repentance

tov — good

tzadeikes — righteous woman

ulpan — Hebrew language lessons

Vilna Gaon — a leading Torah Sage of the eighteenth century

vort — Torah thought

Yaakov — Jacob

yahrtzeit — anniversary of death

Yehudiah — Jewess

Yerushalayim — Jerusalem

Yeshayah — Isaiah

yeshivah bachurim — young men who study at a talmudic seminary

Yid — Jew

Yiddishkeit — Judaism

Yitzchak — Isaac

Yom Kippur — the Day of Atonement

yom tov — holiday

zechus — merit

zt"l — may his memory be blessed